ARUN
LIFEBOATS

An illustrated history of the RNLI Arun class lifeboats 1971–2009

Nicholas Leach

◄ (front cover) The penultimate Arun to be built, 52-45 Mabel Williams, in heavy seas off the west coast of Ireland. (By courtesy of the RNLI)

◄ (frontispiece) 52ft Arun 52-37 Kenneth Thelwall on exercise off Holyhead. (Nicholas Leach)

▲ (this page) 52-43 The Queen Mother off Longhope, Orkney, June 2004. (Nicholas Leach)

ABOUT THIS BOOK

Arun Lifeboats provides a complete history of the class, and contains photographs of all of the Aruns that were built and saw service in the British Isles and Ireland. Part one provides an overview of the history and development of the Arun class. Part two consists of a boat-by-boat guide to each of the Aruns built for the RNLI which served around the UK and Ireland, together with accounts of some of the outstanding rescues. Part three describes what happened to the Aruns after they left RNLI service.

ABOUT THE AUTHOR

Nicholas Leach is Editor of Ships Monthly, Kelsey Publishing's international shipping magazine. He has written extensively about lifeboats and the lifeboat service, including many books on individual lifeboat stations as well as a history of the RNLI's motor lifeboats in 2005. As well as co-authoring and producing guides to lighthouses in England and Wales, he has travelled extensively round the British Isles photographing lifeboats, lighthouses and shipping.

To Sarah

Published by Kelsey Publishing Ltd,
Cudham Tithe Barn, Berry's Hill,
Cudham, Kent TN16 3AG
t > 01959 541444 f > 01959 541400
e > kelseybooks@kelsey.co.uk

ISBN 978-1-907426-21-6
Layout and design by Nicholas Leach
Printed by Pensord, Blackwood

KELSEY PUBLISHING GROUP

Contents

54ft Arun 54-05 B. P. Forties, which served at Aberdeen and
was the first Arun in Scotland. (By courtesy of the RNLI)

▲ 52ft Arun 52-24 Mabel Alice passing Tater-du lighthouse during her time as Penlee lifeboat. (By courtesy of the RNLI)

Acknowledgements

A great many people have conributed to this book, and I am most grateful to them all for their help and assistance. For supplying photographs for possible inclusion, my thanks go to Brian Bevan, Andrew Cooke, Cliff Crone, Tony Denton, Peter Edey, Martin Fish, Ian Leask, Gary Markham, Jon Mathers, John Pagni, Mick Prendergast, Paul Russell and Colin Watson. John O'Regan and Andy Ianetta took me out on their 52ft Aruns in Cork habrour and the Britsol Channel respectively. Around the coast, many lifeboat coxswains and crews, past and present, have assisted and I am particularly grateful to crews at Holyhead, Castletownbere, Donaghadee, Stornoway and Port St Mary lifeboat stations. At the RNLI Headquarters in Poole, thanks to Nathan Williams for supplying photographs, Brian Wead and Valerie Kirsch for launch statistics, and Barry Cox for facilitating my research in the RNLI's library. In Iceland, Sigurður Viðarsson, of ICE-SAR, was extremely helpful in facilitating my visits to Arun lifeboats in his country, as were the Icelandic crews. For proof reading the final version, my thanks to Natasha Singleton. And finally, thank you to Sarah for her support during the writing and preparation of this book.

Nicholas Leach, Lichfield, March 2011

Bibliography

Davies, Joan (1975): Arun Development: a break with tradition to maintain tradition, in *The Lifeboat* (Vol.43, No.451, Spring 1975, pp.286-8).

Dutton, Lt Cdr W. L. G. (1971): 52ft Fast Afloat Boat (FAB) concept, Paper No.12, in Eleventh *International Lifeboat Conference Report*, New York.

Leach, Nicholas (2001): *The Waveney Lifeboats: An illustrated history of the RNLI 44ft Waveney lifeboats 1967-1999* (Bernard McCall, Portishead, Bristol).

Leach, Nicholas (2005): *RNLI Motor Lifeboats* (Landmark, Ashbourne).

Thatcher, Keith (1990): Looking at lifeboats . . . the Arun class, in *The Lifeboat* (Vol.52, No.514, Winter 90/91, p.18-19).

Part One
Arun lifeboat history and development

The Arun class lifeboats were operated by the Royal National Lifeboat Institution (RNLI) from the early 1970s until the twenty-first century, and gave outstanding service. A total of forty-six boats of the class were built and served at stations throughout the British Isles and Ireland. Upon replacement, many were sold abroad to foreign lifeboat societies and continue the work of sea rescue around the world, notably in China, Iceland and Finland, showing the Arun to be a design of true longevity and excellence.

The development of the Arun can be traced back to the early 1960s, when the RNLI was looking to introduce faster offshore lifeboats into the fleet. A fast lifeboat, 64ft in length and named *Sir William Hillary*, had been built in 1929 for service at Dover, but this was a one-off craft. Designed to help ditched aircraft in the English Channel, she was powered by twin 375hp engines and could reach speeds of more than seventeen knots, considerably faster than any motor lifeboat built hitherto. She spent a decade on station at Dover, saving twenty-nine lives, and would have served the RNLI for longer had the Second World War not intervened, with the Admiralty taking her over in October 1940 for their use. Once she had left the fleet, the RNLI did not build any lifeboats which could go faster than ten knots for more than two decades.

The lifeboat fleet of the post-war era and the 1950s was made up entirely of displacement wooden-hulled lifeboats, sturdy and rugged craft capable of,

▼ The fine sight of a 52ft Arun at speed, as Roy and Barbara Harding returns to station at Castletownbere following exercise. (Nicholas Leach)

► The 52ft Barnett Ramsay-Dyce (ON.944) was typical of the RNLI's post-1945 fleet of displacement wooden-hulled designs, which were eventually replaced by the Aruns. Powered by twin 72hp engines, she could reach a top speed of nine knots, was not self-righting, and offered only basic protection for her crew. (Grahame Farr, by courtesy of the RNLI)

► The 44ft Waveney Arthur and Blanche Harris (ON.1005), which served at Barry Dock, Donaghadee and Courtmacsherry Harbour, pictured on trials shortly after being built. She was one of twenty-two Waveney lifeboats built by the RNLI, and the fifth of six boats constructed by Brooke Marine at Lowestoft in the late 1960s. (From an old photo in the author's collection)

at best, a little over nine knots. Between 1945 and 1960 over 100 new motor lifeboats were constructed, an average of eight per annum. However, these new boats, of the Watson, Barnett and Liverpool types, were based on a hull design from the nineteenth century, albeit built to a larger scale and fitted with the latest equipment, basic diesel engines and twin screws. Some improvements had been implemented in the post-war years, such as the introduction of a midship-steering position in the larger Watson classes, and a policy of fitting all lifeboats with diesel engines was pursued. But in general, the RNLI's approach to new lifeboat design was somewhat cautious, and trusted methods and materials were preferred to innovation and new technology.

A number of factors contributed towards the relative lack of innovation in lifeboat design at this time. First, the RNLI believed that new and relatively untried ideas and equipment should not be introduced into the lifeboat service. Indeed, in 1947 the RNLI's Chief Inspector of Lifeboats, Commander P. E. Vaux, stated that 'a lifeboat is not the medium to experiment with', and added that every part of a lifeboat should be 'thoroughly tested and proved to the hilt'. Second, two-thirds of the fleet of 160 boats were launched either down slipways or from carriages, and it was the RNLI's policy that lifeboats should, as far as possible, be interchangeable. Accordingly, nearly all boats were capable of being launched down a slipway. This meant a standard midship section and hull form with the propellers in tunnels, to protect them during recovery up a slipway and prevent cavitation. And thirdly, it was believed that fast craft were not as seaworthy as the slower traditional displacement lifeboats.

But by the early 1960s, when it was apparent that the pattern of casualties was changing and that future lifeboat work would be more about assisting recreational craft rather than merchant vessels and fishing boats, getting to casualties faster became a significant factor in lifeboat and life-saving technology. Some initial resistance was shown among volunteer crews and RNLI staff to the introduction of faster lifeboats, but this was gradually lessened when it was realised that faster boats could be built without sacrificing the sea-keeping qualities of the older designs. Moreover, it was seen as necessary to have faster lifeboats to enable the RNLI's fleet to be deployed to the best advantage, both operationally and economically. As well as faster all-weather lifeboats, the small inflatable inshore lifeboat (ILB) was introduced during the 1960s. It played a major part in shaping the modern lifeboat fleet, became of key importance to saving lives at sea.

The first design of faster all-weather lifeboat, the 44ft Waveney class, entered service in 1966 and, according to the RNLI Naval Architect Keith Thatcher, 'proved to be an unqualified success'. The Waveney was based on a US Coast Guard design developed in the late 1950s, and when introduced in UK waters it was the first time the RNLI had seriously considered putting a fast lifeboat into service on a widespread basis around the country. However, the RNLI did not initially consider the Waveney to be a true all-weather lifeboat, although the outstanding services undertaken by the boats in all conditions proved this to be an incorrect assumption. So in the 1960s, encouraged by the reception received on the coast by the Waveneys, the RNLI looked at designing a larger, but somewhat faster, self-righting lifeboat, capable of speeds in excess of eighteen knots.

In 1969 a specification was drawn up for a twenty-knot boat, fully self-righting, with an all-weather capability, of about 52ft in length and a draught of 4ft 9in. Other requirements were for the boat to lie afloat at moorings and the design to

▼ Model tank testing the Arun hull during the design and development work. (By courtesy of the RNLI)

be suitable for eventual construction in glass reinforced plastic (GRP). It was decided to aim for a hull form that offered development potential, although for the prototype boat to have a speed of about eighteen knots was considered satisfactory. These, together with the standard requirements arising from considerations of seaworthiness, efficiency and low building and maintenance costs, formed the criteria to be fulfilled. Two requirements were a substantial departure from the conventional British nine knot lifeboat: namely, the possible construction in GRP, and the speed of eighteen knots. Using GRP for lifeboat construction made economic sense to the RNLI because of the ever increasing cost of building in more conventional materials such as wood and steel.

Construction of the boats in GRP created a number of technical problems which were beyond the experience of the RNLI, and as the proposed design was such a radical departure from conventional lifeboat development, an outside firm of naval architects was engaged to prepare a set of plans. Messrs G. L. Watson, of Glasgow, was commissioned to prepare the hull design, and their designer, Alan McLachlan, produced plans for a 52ft semi-displacement hull with soft bilges and multiple spray rails at the waterline. The deep-V monohedron hull had a transom stern, but a round bilge form was retained and shallow tunnels were incorporated to afford some protection for the propellers. An inherent self-righting capability was provided through the hull shape and large wheelhouse, which was designed to act as an integral part of the boat's reserve buoyancy and be, in effect, a large watertight compartment, forcing the boat to right in the event of a capsize.

The general arrangement, superstructure layout and machinery were formulated by the RNLI's technical staff, who oversaw the vessel's construction process. Early in 1970 a model of the design was subjected to a series of tank tests at the Experimental and Electronics Laboratories of the British Hovercraft Corporation at East Cowes, Isle of Wight. The model showed that the design had good sea-keeping qualities and was difficult to capsize in the worst simulated conditions. But the model tests indicated changes were needed to improve performance, and so the RNLI's staff redrew the lines to incorporate extra beam and tunnels to allow larger propellers. The multiple spray rails were also removed as they increased, rather than suppressed, the amount of spray taken on board.

The material chosen for the first of the class was laminated wood with three skins of agba on laminated timber frames, a conventional boatbuilding method.

► The interior layout of the prototype Arun, 52-01, showing the various crew positions and navigational equipment that was carried when the boat was newly built. Inside the wheelhouse were seats, with safety belts and arm rests, for each member of the crew, with special positions for the coxswain, navigator, radio operator, mechanic and crew members, as well as provision for a doctor. The two survivors' cabins below deck contained rescue equipment including first aid gear, stretchers, emergency rations and blankets.
(By courtesy of the RNLI)

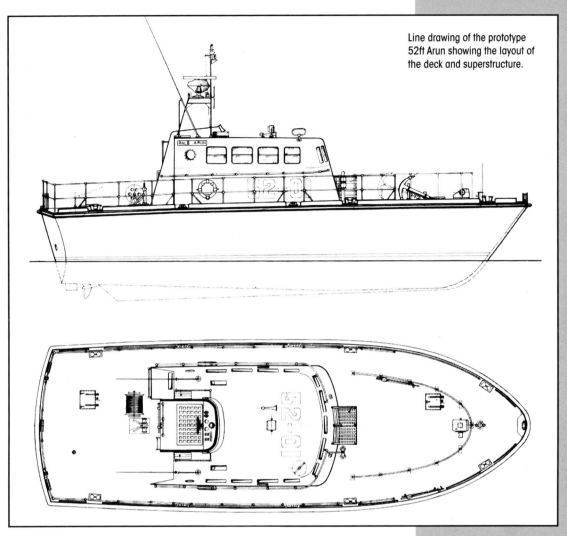

The hull contained twenty-four watertight compartments, and a double bottom extended throughout its length. An inner skin was formed to the sides of the boat and the resultant void, together with the double bottom, was filled with expanded foam polyurethane to give the boat enough buoyancy to keep it afloat even if all the watertight spaces were holed. The decking, longitudinal and transverse bulkheads, inner skin, and bottom were all made from mahogany plywood, and transverse bulkheads subdivided the boat into six main watertight sections: forepeak, anchor cable locker, fore cabin, engine room, after cabin and steerage flat. Although the hull design was capable of speeds up to twenty-eight knots, with the machinery installed in the prototype a maximum speed of 19.95 knots was achieved.

The prototype boat, named *Arun*, official number (ON) 1018 and operational number 52-01, was commissioned from William Osborne Ltd of Littlehampton, a company with a long history of building for the RNLI and with experience of constructing prototype lifeboats. The new boat was laid down in February 1970 and was launched in March 1971. On 19 April 1971 she was demonstrated to the press with Rear Admiral Sir Edmund Irving KBE, a member of the RNLI's committee of management, on hand to describe the boat in detail. Not only was the boat named *Arun*, but the class was designated the Arun class after the river

▲ The prototype 52ft Arun, named Arun, on trials. Many coxswains and crews tried her and all were highly enthusiastic about her seakeeping and handling capabilities. A few older crew were initially sceptical about the drastic change of shape and appearance in comparison to the 'traditional' lifeboats and expressed concern about the exposed screws and rudders. However, a short trip afloat soon removed any doubts. (By courtesy of the RNLI)

in Littlehampton where the first boat was built. The RNLI formulated a policy in the 1970s of naming lifeboat classes after rivers rather than lifeboat designers, so in place of the Watson, Barnett and Oakley types, the fleet comprised Waveney, Rother, Solent, Clyde and Thames types during the 1970s and 1980s.

With the completion of the prototype, the RNLI designers realised that the operational evaluation of the boat would highlight shortcomings in both the design and general arrangement, which could be corrected in a second boat. Only when the design had fully proved itself would consideration be given to construction in GRP. So the prototype, after a period of extensive evaluation along the south coast, was taken on a tour of the British Isles starting in June 1971 with a call at the capital. She was in London between 22 and 25 June 1971, berthed at Lambeth Bridge, where she was shown to interested parties. She left London and continued her evaluation trials, calling at Harwich on 26 June, Gorleston the following day and at Spurn on 28 June, with an overnight stop in Grimsby. She then travelled extensively round the British Isles, calling at stations in Scotland, Ireland and Wales, so that crews could see her at first hand.

The prototype 52-01 continued her tour round the country until, on 23 October 1971, she left Littlehampton and went south to Spain, as a Spanish Red Cross delegation was investigating the organisational structure of the RNLI and looking at various different types of lifeboat. The Spanish organisation was newly established and, in its infancy, had turned to the RNLI for assistance in getting up and running. The passage south took *Arun* to La Coruna via St Peter Port, Brest, La Pallais, Santander and Gijon. A 46ft 6in Solent class lifeboat had also visited Spain, and so *Arun* was the second British lifeboat to go to the country that year. While in Spain, the sea trials undertaken on *Arun* continued and familiarisation exercises were undertaken with a Spanish crew on board.

Cutaway drawing of prototype 52ft Arun 52-01 ON.1018

Key: (1) Inflatable dinghy, (2) Aft cabin with galley, (3) Flying bridge, (4) Radio/radar operator, (5) Coxswain's seat, (6) Watertight hatch to forward cabin, (7) Navigator's position, (8) Rope stowage, (9) Emergency life raft, (10) Forward cabin, (11) Cable locker, (12) Polyurethane foam buoyancy, (13) Petter generator set, (14) Two 375bhp Caterpillar D336 diesel engines, (15) Fuel tanks port and starboard, each of 259 gallons, (16) Coffer dam entrance to wheelhouse to prevent flooding if boat capsizes.

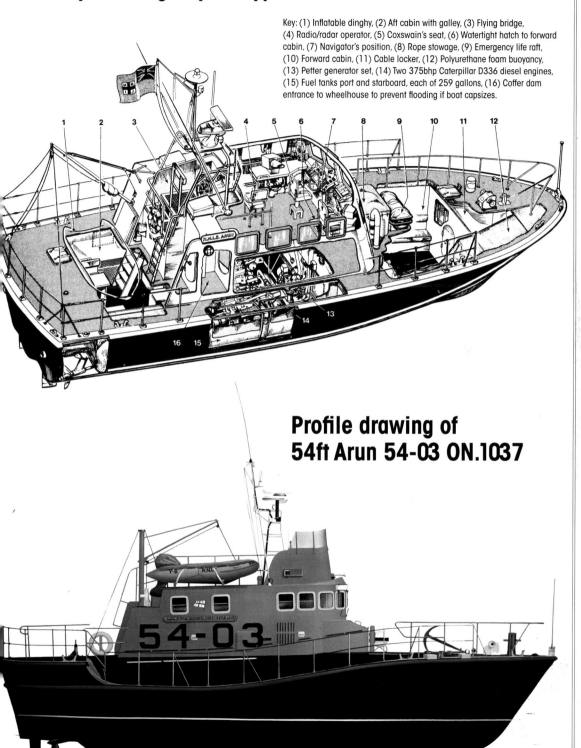

Profile drawing of 54ft Arun 54-03 ON.1037

Between 29 and 31 May 1972 52-01 was taken to Sweden to participate in an international conference of voluntary lifeboat organisations. She was used to take the RNLI delegation to Sweden, and visited ports in the Netherlands, Germany, Denmark and Norway on her way north. On her return, she was used for operational duties at Kirkwall, in Orkney, while that station's 70ft Clyde class lifeboat *Grace Paterson Ritchie* was being surveyed. *Arun* then went back to Littlehampton, where she was based during her the rest of her evaluation trials.

While the prototype was being taken round Britain and Ireland, as well as further afield, work on the second and third boats was under way. The second boat incorporated significant changes above the waterline. While the prototype was found to be a good sea boat, one of the main disadvantages was her high freeboard. So the second prototype had her deck line lowered amidships, making it easier to recover survivors from the water, and as a result the sheerline was cut down to give 3ft of freeboard amidships. A redesigned wheelhouse was also introduced, providing two separate cabins above deck, and the engines were also uprated to give enhanced performance. An inflatable shallow water inflatable rescue boat, designated the Y class, was carried on a gantry over the after deck with its own launching crane. The prototype Arun had the flying bridge, which incorporated an upper steering position, at the rear of the superstructure, and the second boat had the flying bridge in a similar position on the superstructure.

This second boat, named *Sir William Arnold* with the operational number 52-02, was launched in spring 1973. After initial trials during June, she was sent to the Guernsey station of St Peter Port for further evaluation throughout July, before returning to Littlehampton for minor modifications. She then went back to Guernsey in November 1973 and, after a period of crew training, was placed on station there the same month. She was named by HRH the Duchess of Kent at St Peter Port on 23 May 1974 as part of the first visit to Guernsey by the Duchess. She went on to undertake a large number of rescues, many of which involved her crew showing outstanding courage and bravery and resulted in the awarding of numerous medals for gallantry, described below.

With the first two prototypes on extensive evaluation trials, work on the third boat was under way. This boat had a further change to the hull, which was lengthened to 54ft having had the transom corners radiused to produce an elliptical stern. It was believed that this would give better handling in following seas and also make the corners of the transom less vulnerable. The construction material used was again laminated timber, identical to 52-01 and 52-02, and the boat was completed in 1975 as 54-03, allocated to Brixham as the Torbay lifeboat, and named *Edward Bridges (Civil Service & Post Office No.37)*.

Edward Bridges was launched from Osborne's yard in October 1974 and was used for extensive trials and evaluation between then and January 1975. Her hull, although longer, had the same cut away sheerline as 52-02, but the wheelhouse was again revised, with the flying bridge located forward to improve the helm's degree of visibility and the Y class inflatable was placed behind it, on a cradle mounted on the rear of the superstructure. The second and third Aruns had more powerful engines than the prototype, and the intention was that they would achieve twenty-two or twenty-three knots, which was considered sufficient, but in practice they did not reach much more than twenty knots.

Following the launch of the third wooden boat, the RNLI began to consider production using glass reinforced plastic (GRP). Considerable thought was given to GRP construction and the RNLI was able to call on much expert advice. It had always been the intention to build the bulk of the Arun class using GRP and so

◀The first 54ft Arun, and last of the boats to be built from wood, 54-03 Edward Bridges pictured off Orkney during her trials and evaluation circumnavigation. She was one of many lifeboats to be funded by the Civil Service Lifeboat Fund. (By courtesy of the RNLI)

a mould was constructed based on the hull of the latest boat, 54-03, but slightly modified to suit the new material. Since the users of the boats had not been able to decide which stern configuration was best, the mould was given a removable stern section to allow 52ft and 54ft boats to be built as required. This mould was subsequently used for every Arun hull, apart from one, all of which were produced by Halmatic, at Havant, near Portsmouth.

The first GRP-hulled boat was *Tony Vandervell*, operation number 54-04 (ON.1049), which was fitted out at William Osborne's yard between June 1974 and July 1975 and then taken on evaluation trials. During July 1975 she was taken on a tour of lifeboat stations to assess her performance. Only one other lifeboat before her had been moulded from GRP, the 40ft Keith Nelson *Ernest William and Elizabeth Ellen Hinde* (ON.1017), which had been completed in 1969 as an experimental boat using a commercial hull and layout design by the Keith Nelson company. No other boats of this type were built, but *Ernest William and Elizabeth Ellen Hinde* went on to enjoy a fine career, serving fifteen years at the Calshot station covering Southampton Water and the entrance to the Solent.

To complement the GRP hull of 54-04, Halmatic developed a superstructure made from GRP, which was almost identical in shape to the aluminium alloy wheelhouse fitted to 54-03. In general the change was successful, but the GRP structure proved slightly heavier and caused problems with radio reception and the communications equipment, as GRP has little or no 'shielding' effect. A decision was therefore taken to revert to an aluminium wheelhouse for the ninth Arun, 52-09 *Spirit of Tayside* (ON.1056) and the shape remained constant from then on. With the eighth boat, 52-08 *Joy and John Wade* (ON.1053), the 52ft hull with transom stern was reintroduced, and the hull shape then remained unchanged for the remainder of the build programme.

◄ 54ft Arun Edward Bridges (Civil Service and Post Office No.37) pictured at Plymouth in July 1974 taking part in the International Lifeboat Exhibition, which was held during the RNLI's 150th anniversary year. (Grahame Farr, by courtesy of the RNLI)

By the mid-1970s, when the 52ft design had been settled upon, the RNLI had realised that the Arun was an excellent lifeboat and was well suited to all-weather service throughout the Institution's area of responsibility, from the Atlantic swell on the west coast of Ireland to the south coast of England, the North Sea and the northern archipelagos of Orkney and Shetland. From an initial reluctance by crews to accept the new design, the Arun became one of the mainstays of the RNLI's fleet during the 1980s and 1990s. And the view was taken that the RNLI's tradition of life-saving at sea was being upheld: 'a break with tradition to maintain tradition', according to *The Lifeboat* journal of spring 1975.

During the late 1970s the Arun building programme was well under way and by 1980 twelve boats of the class had been placed on station. The seventh boat, and the last of the 54ft hulled Aruns, was sent to the important Humber station at Spurn Point. Named *City of Bradford IV* (ON.1052), she arrived at Spurn in March 1977 and was placed on a mooring in the river. Reaching the new boat at the moorings was initially problematic, but the provision of a suitable boarding boat, powered by outboard engines, which could be safely launched from the Pilot Jetty at Spurn, overcame the difficulties.

The problems of acceptable boarding arrangements had been an issue when the RNLI first considered building boats which could only be kept afloat, as opposed

◄ The prototype Arun lifeboats were built of wood, with the intention of future construction in glass-reinforced plastic once the necessary lessons from the first prototype had been learned. For the first of the GRP boats a wooden plug was prepared from which the mould was constructed. This mould, pictured at Halmatic's yard at Havant, Hampshire, was first used for Weymouth's Arun 54-04 Tony Vandervell. (By courtesy of the RNLI)

►The hull of 54-04, the first GRP Arun to be constructed, in William Osborne's yard at Littlehampton. (By courtesy of the RNLI)

►The hull of 54-04 is lowered into the river Arun at Littlehampton by crane. (By courtesy of the RNLI)

►The hull of 54-04, the first GRP lifeboat, is lowered into the river Arun at Littlehampton by crane and is floated for the first time. (By courtesy of the RNLI)

to in a boathouse, as had an apparent paucity of places where suitable harbours existed. However, whereas the favoured method of launching had once been the slipway, keeping lifeboats afloat became the norm once the Aruns started entering service. The first Aruns were sent to stations where the lifeboat being replaced had been on a mooring, with Humber being the first station where a slipway-launched boat was replaced by an Arun. But by the 1980s more stations that employed slipway launching were allocated Aruns, and at Broughty Ferry, Tynemouth, Portrush, St Mary's and Fishguard suitable berths were found so that an Arun could be kept afloat, whereas previously a boathouse and slipway had been used. This policy of changing from slipway launching to afloat berths has, over time, led to a significant reduction in the number of slipway launched lifeboats, and in Scotland, by the end of the Arun build programme, only a handful of stations employed slipway launching.

All Aruns except for the three wood prototypes had been built in GRP, and the GRP boats were in production when, in the 1980s, a decision was made to experiment with steel production. The thirtieth boat of the class, *Snolda* (ON.1100), had a steel hull with aluminium alloy decks and her operational number of 52-030 carried the extra zero to denote steel construction. She was built by Fairey Marine in 1985 as part of an investigation into building the remaining boats from this material. The experiment proved a complete success and many coxswains considered 52-030 to be the best Arun for comfort and handling. However, the relatively high cost of the boat's construction ended the prospect of more Aruns being built in steel, as they would have cost almost half as much again as the GRP-hulled boats.

Within a decade of entering service, the Arun had proved itself time and again in difficult circumstances, with some outstanding rescues being undertaken in the boats by the RNLI's volunteer crews, and in 1982 a Design Council Award was

▲ The first Arun to be moulded from glass reinforced plastic was 54-04 Tony Vandervell, pictured at Weymouth. The boat contained nearly a ton of polyeruthane buoyancy foam, six tons of glass fibre and three tons of polyester resin in her hull, deck and superstructure. The hull was built by Halmatic and the whole project was completed in eighteen months.

▲ The Port St Mary
Arun lifeboat, 54-06
The Gough-Ritchie, on
exercise off the Isle of
Man with an RAF rescue
helicopter. (By courtesy of
Port St Mary RNLI)

presented to the RNLI for the hull shape and overall design of the boat, the first lifeboat to achieve such recognition. At the naming ceremony of the relief Arun 52-20 *Duchess of Kent* (ON.1077) in London on 27 April 1982, Rear Admiral W. J. Graham, the RNLI director, said that 'the Arun is an outstanding success story; three of the last four gold medal awards have been for services carried out in Arun class lifeboats and I can reveal that the Arun class has been awarded a 1982 Design Council Award'. The award was presented the day after the ceremony by HRH The Duke of Edinburgh on board *Duchess of Kent*.

The speed and range of the Aruns enabled a much faster response time to incidents, many of which would have been beyond the range of the previous lifeboats. Some outstanding services were undertaken by lifeboat crews in Aruns and by the time the Arun's design had been formally recognised by the Design Council, three gold medal-winning rescues had been performed in Aruns. The first of these was in 1976 by the Torbay crew, just over a year after they received the third Arun, *Edward Bridges,* with the dramatic and daring rescue going a long way to proving, if proof were needed, the outstanding nature of the Arun design.

The service started in the early hours of 6 December 1976 when *Edward Bridges* was called out to help the motor vessel *Lyrma,* which had steering gear failure and had developed a list. Under Second Coxswain Keith Bower, the lifeboat headed out in southerly force nine to ten winds, with the crew secured inside and all doors and hatches closed. The lifeboat was able to steam at full speed, nearly nineteen knots, in only a slight to moderate sea eastwards towards Berry Head. But as the lifeboat rounded the headland, huge seas were encountered, forcing Acting Coxswain Bower to ease the throttles drastically. The largest waves were estimated at 40ft high, the worst conditions ever experienced by the crew. Acting Coxswain Bower needed all his skills to prevent the boat from becoming airborne too often and from pounding too hard as the sea conditions worsened. All except three of the lifeboat's crew suffered seasickness on the passage, but all continued to perform their duties.

After an hour and a half at sea contact was made with the casualty, which was just over seven miles from Start Point. The wind had reached force ten to eleven, and effecting a rescue was considered impossible by Bower. Two other vessels were standing by while *Lyrma*, listing heavily to starboard, was slowly steaming in a circle, pitching and rolling so that her well deck was awash, with the captain fearing a further shift of cargo would capsize her. He wanted everyone taken off. An attempt was made by a Wessex helicopter from RFA *Engadine*, but this had to be aborted after the winchman, having been lowered over *Lyrma's* aft superstructure, was caught up in a davit and injured.

So, with no hope of rescue other than the lifeboat, Acting Coxswain Bower decided to make a trial run on to the casualty's starboard quarter to assess the possibilities. When the trial run proved successful, the captain agreed to muster his crew on the starboard side aft to be taken off. On the first run alongside, the only woman passenger was successfully pulled aboard. The lifeboat then went astern and tried again. This time the motion between the two vessels forced Bower to come hard astern at the last minute to avoid a collision. On the next approach two more survivors were pulled aboard, but on the next approach only one could be got aboard before Bower was forced to withdraw. Another abortive approach followed, then the sixth run was begun.

As the lifeboat's port bow came alongside, *Lyrma* rolled heavily to starboard, crushing nine guardrail stanchions inboard and sending the lifeboatmen leaping for safety over the pulpit rail as the guardrail bolts sheered. The lifeboat was

◄The relief 52ft Arun 52-20 *Duchess of Kent* on duty at Bary Dock. The Design Council Award given to the RNLI in recognition of the outstanding nature of the Arun design was presented on board this Arun in 1982. (Phil Weeks)

KEEP SHUT AT SEA

▶ The engine room of 54-07 City of Bradford IV, showing the twin 460hp Caterpillar D343 diesels. (By courtesy of the RNLI)

trapped under the casualty's gunwales and the freighter rolled down on top of her, enabling Assistant Mechanic John Hunkin, standing beside Bower on the upper steering position, to lean over to fend off the casualty's lifeboat, still in its davits, about five feet inboard of *Lyrma*. One more survivor jumped to the lifeboat's deck, but another hesitated forcing crewman John Dew to come forward over the pulpit rails and drag the man to safety, as Bower put both engines full astern and the lifeboat was brought free of the casualty.

On the next run, the seventh crew man came aboard and this left only the captain, who shouted that the other two crew members had taken to the life raft over the port bow. It took two more runs, however, before he could be taken aboard. During this entire evacuation, the Wessex helicopter stood by and the pilot said that he considered the lifeboat crew displayed 'fantastic seamanship', as he did not believe it possible to get anyone off safely by lifeboat in the conditions. The lifeboat was then manoeuvred to windward of *Lyrma* and the lifeboatmen picked up the two occupants of the life raft. Acting Coxswain Bower turned to port to make a lee as the last of the ten survivors was pulled safely aboard over

the lifeboat's starboard side. It was just after 4am and the survivors were placed inside the lifeboat and the aft door was closed.

Bower and Hunkin remained on the upper steering position during the passage back to station as they could see the large following seas better from that position, and take any action necessary to prevent broaching. Visibility had improved by this time, so that navigating visually from the upper bridge position was possible and full speed was maintained all the way home. The lifeboat reached her berth at 5.10am having completed a momentous rescue. In recognition of the skill, seamanship and outstanding bravery displayed, the gold medal was awarded to Acting Coxswain Keith Bower, and bronze medals were awarded to Mechanic Stephen Bower, Assistant Mechanic John Hunkin and crew members John Dew, Michael Mills, Nicholas Davies and Richard Brown.

At the Humber, the seventh Arun to be built, *City of Bradford IV* (ON.1052), and her crew, led by Superintendent Coxswain Brian Bevan, hit the national headlines during the winter of 1978-79 when they undertook three dramatic rescues in quick succession, all of which resulted in formal recognition for Coxswain Bevan. *City of Bradford IV* was manned by the RNLI's only full-time paid crew and they became well-known figures after the boat was involved in three medal-winning services, one of which saw Bevan awarded the gold medal, the second such award for a rescue in an Arun.

The first of these services took place on 30 December 1978 when the Dutch coaster *Diana V* got into difficulties seventy-four miles south-east of Spurn Point. *City of Bradford IV* put out at 2.10pm with Coxswain Brian Bevan at the helm. As she cleared the river, she ran into extremely heavy seas, whipped up by a violent easterly gale, with visibility reduced at times to less than 100 yards. At 4pm as Coxswain Bevan headed at full speed into the violent seas, having by then covered about twenty-five miles, *City of Bradford IV* suddenly lost speed after an oil supply pipe fractured, as a result of the pounding that the boat had been taking. Knowing that HMS *Lindisfarne* was standing by the casualty and that the Cromer lifeboat

was on her way, Coxswain Bevan decided to return to Grimsby for repairs. The lifeboat's two mechanics then worked as fast as they could to replace the damaged pipe and by 9.36pm the lifeboat was on her way to the casualty again.

City of Bradford IV headed towards *Diana V*, with HMS *Lindisfarne* reporting that the situation was getting worse. The lifeboat battled her way through 25ft waves, which battered both boat and crew, heading almost directly into the short, steep seas at full speed, at times taking off and crashing into the next wave. At 10.35pm, when still eight miles from the casualty, she crashed down from an exceptionally large sea and all lighting, window wipers and fans failed. Crew member Dennis Bailey, Jnr, was thrown against the wheelhouse bulkhead and injured. Speed had to be reduced to ten knots to give the mechanics a chance to find the fault and restore the lighting.

While repairs were being made, HMS *Lindisfarne* radioed that the lifeboat was urgently needed to take off the coaster's four crew and two women, so Coxswain Bevan resumed at full speed. The coaster was reached at 11pm and the lifeboat prepared to go alongside *Diana V*, which had a heavy list and was steering erratically. With the wind at storm force ten gusting to fifty-six knots, the lifeboatmen tied fenders round the lifeboat's bow. As they worked on the foredeck, heavy seas repeatedly swept over them and, with the air temperature at minus four degrees centigrade, the sea froze on the deck and handrails.

With the crew of HMS *Lindisfarne* illuminating the scene with their searchlight, Coxswain Bevan took the lifeboat towards the coaster. All the lifeboatmen, except for Bevan and the two mechanics, were on the foredeck, with their lifelines fastened to the rails. As the lifeboat edged towards the coaster's port quarter, a heavy breaking sea struck *Diana V*, almost washing the crew off deck. The two vessels were smashed together, and part of the lifeboat's rubbing strake was ripped away with the anchor-stowage damaged. With the lifeboat's bow then 10ft above the coaster's deck, Coxswain Bevan put both engines full astern and pulled *City of Bradford IV* clear. A second approach was made, but this time a very heavy sea struck the lifeboat, smashing her starboard bow against the coaster with such force that one of the fenders exploded and more of the rubbing strake was torn away. As the coaster heeled right over, she was only 3ft from Coxswain Bevan, who was on the lifeboat's flying bridge. Again he quickly put the engines into reverse and the lifeboat pulled clear.

Build programme summary

Various changes were made during the Arun build programme, as the design was developed and modified. The following is a summary of the changes:

52-01 Flying bridge aft on superstructure, with straight freeboard; powered by twin Caterpillar TA 0336 diesel engines.

52-02 Flying bridge aft on superstructure, freeboard cut away to aid survivor recovery; powered by twin Caterpillar TA 343 marine diesels, each developing 460bhp at 2,000rpm, operating through two-to-one reduction gearboxes and each fitted with two ninety-amp alternators.

52-01, 52-02, 54-03 The three prototypes had wooden laminate hulls, and were assembled complete by William Osborne Ltd at Littlehampton, Sussex.

54-03, 54-04, 54-05, 54-06, 54-07 Five boats built 2ft longer to be 54ft in length, having a rounded transom, indicated by the operational number 54. Earlier and subsequent boats had

a square transom and were 52ft in length.

54-04 From the fourth boat onwards, all boats were GRP hulled with the hulls moulded by Halmatic Ltd, at Havant, and fitted out by the builder listed.

52-08 The first boat to have a square transom, giving a length of 52ft, as used in all subsequent boats.

52-10 Aluminium alloy wheelhouse reintroduced from 1979

52-11 Wheelhouse layout redesigned, open plan introduced.

52-030 Steel-hulled construction, but only one steel boat built, assembled complete at Cowes.

52-43 Hull laminate was changed to epacryn resin from 1988 for the last four boats.

52-46 Last 52ft Arun to be built, completed in 1990.

Equipment In addition to standard radio and other electronic equipment, Aruns were fitted with Decca Mk.101 Super Radar, Decca Navigator Mk.21, and Decca Automatic Pilot Type 350.

On the third run, the lifeboat's bow hit the coaster about 5ft below where the crew were huddled and a twelve-year-old girl was dropped into the arms of the waiting lifeboatmen. Then, as the lifeboat rose on the top of the following wave, a woman and four men jumped across. The lifeboat's engines were put full astern and she pulled clear with the six survivors, who were wet, cold and suffering from shock. Coxswain Bevan brought the lifeboat round again to take up station on the coaster's port quarter as the master, his crew safe, had decided to stay on board to try and save his ship.

Escorted by the lifeboat and HMS *Lindisfarne*, *Diana V* then limped towards the Humber, twenty miles away, huge waves repeatedly sweeping her. She struggled on and entered the Humber just before 2am, a pilot went on board and *City of Bradford IV* was able to return to Spurn, where ambulances were waiting to take the survivors to hospital. The lifeboat had been at sea for nearly fourteen hours in truly appalling conditions. For his outstanding seamanship, great courage and fine leadership, Superintendent Coxswain Bevan was awarded a silver medal. For their courage and bravery during this extremely demanding service, the Thanks Inscribed on Vellum were awarded to each of the other members of that gallant crew: Second Coxswain Dennis Bailey, snr, Motor Mechanic Barry Sayers, Assistant Mechanic Ronald Sayers and lifeboatmen Michael B. Storey, Peter Jordan and Dennis Bailey, Jnr.

Just six weeks after this dramatic service, the Humber lifeboatmen performed an even more dramatic rescue after the Panamanian motor vessel *Revi* was reported in distress thirty miles north-east of Spurn Point. Just after midnight on 14 February 1979 *City of Bradford IV* slipped her moorings and headed out into extremely rough seas and a north-easterly gale, with gusts up to force nine and increasing. By the time the lifeboat had cleared the river and was about two miles north-east of Spurn light vessel, she was heading into very large seas. She crested

▲ 52-08 Joy and John Wade being boarded by her crew at Yarmouth prior to leaving on service. She was the first Arun to have a square transom, but one of the last to have a bulkhead in the wheelhouse. (Paul Russell)

one and then fell fifteen to twenty feet, hitting the next trough so hard that the electric breakers on the lights and window wipers opened. Speed was reduced to fourteen knots in the head seas, which were now estimated to be thirty-five feet high. The lifeboat arrived on scene at 1.36am and found *Revi* heading slowly towards the Humber. Heavy following seas were lifting the coaster's stern out of the water, while her bows were constantly being buried.

Revi slowed down so that two of the crew could be taken off, something which Coxswain Bevan initially thought would be impossible in the conditions. But he instructed *Revi* to steer south at slow speed and to have the two men on the boat deck on her starboard quarter, ready to jump. Bevan then slowly took the lifeboat towards the coaster but just as she came under the casualty's starboard quarter, a huge wave struck *Revi*, completely covering her stern and sending her crashing down towards the lifeboat. Coxswain Bevan put both engines full astern and the lifeboat pulled clear, just avoiding being damaged. Nine attempts then had to be made before the two men were successfully taken off *Revi*, whose stern at times was twenty-five feet above the lifeboat. The two men eventually jumped to safety as the lifeboat came up to *Revi* in blinding snow.

But five minutes later the situation started deteriorating rapidly with the ship's accommodation flooding and the cargo shifting, leaving the vessel with a forty-five degree list. *Revi's* master realised he had to abandon ship so he turned *Revi* to provide a lee for the lifeboat on the port side, while the lifeboatmen moved the fenders to the other side, a difficult task in the violent seas with huge waves repeatedly sweeping them. As the lifeboat came alongside on the first approach, a large wave broke over both boats and swept the lifeboat away from the ship. The same thing happened again and again and it took about another twelve attempts before the lifeboat could be brought alongside at a moment when, with a reasonable height between the two decks, a man was able to jump.

The mate jumped six feet into the arms of the lifeboat's crew who broke his fall and hurried him below. *Revi's* bows were now almost submerged and her stern was clear of the water, at times hanging dangerously above the lifeboat. The last survivor, the master, was hanging on to the outside of *Revi's* stern rails, ready to jump. On about the tenth attempt to get him off, as *City of Bradford IV* approached *Revi's* quarter, the stricken vessel's stern rose twenty feet in the air and began to crash down towards the lifeboat's foredeck, where the crew were

► A fine photograph of the 54ft Arun 54-04 City of Bradford IV off Spurn Point. She was used during the winter of 1978-79 to perform some of the most daring and difficult services ever undertake by RNLI lifeboats. (By courtesy of Brian Bevan)

lashed to the rails with little or no chance to get clear. Seeing what was happening, Coxswain Bevan rammed the throttles full astern and the Arun's impressive power pulled her clear with only inches and seconds to spare.

As they prepared to go in again, three enormous waves completely covered *Revi* and it was feared that the master had been lost, but when the water cleared he was seen clinging desperately to the stern rails. Coxswain Bevan realised that *Revi* was now on the point of capsizing, so he took the lifeboat through a trough between two waves and under the coaster's port quarter, striking her stern, giving the master the chance to jump. He almost fell overboard as he leapt to safety, but the lifeboatmen just managed to grab him and haul him aboard. Just minutes later, *Revi* rolled over and sank. Coxswain Bevan set course for Grimsby where the survivors were landed and the lifeboat left at 6.09am to be back on her moorings at Spurn just over an hour later.

For this truly outstanding rescue, during which the lifeboat had to be manoeuvred up to *Revi* thirty-five times, in the most appalling conditions, Superintendent Coxswain Bevan was awarded the gold medal. It had also been a service demanding great skill and tremendous courage on the part of the whole gallant crew and bronze medals were awarded to each of the other men, Second Coxswain Dennis Bailey, snr, Mechanic Barry Sayers, Assistant Mechanic Ronald Sayers and lifeboatmen Michael Story, Peter Jordan, Sydney Rollinson and Dennis Bailey, Jnr.

The day after this remarkable rescue, 15 February 1979, *City of Bradford IV* went out once again and, in the same severe weather that she faced when she went to *Revi*, completed another outstanding service. The casualty on this occasion was the Romanian cargo vessel *Savinesti*, with twenty-eight people on board, which was in distress thirty-seven miles south-east of Spurn Point. The Wells lifeboat *Ernest Tom Neathercoat*, a 37ft Oakley type with an open steering position, was launched at 10.24am and encountered exceptionally heavy seas churned up by the violent north-easterly gale, and conditions were extremely cold with frequent snow storms. The lifeboat was hit repeatedly by enormous breaking seas and she was labouring heavily to clear the huge volume of water she was taking on board. Help was needed from the Arun, which with her enclosed wheelhouse gave the crew the necessary level of protection.

Just boarding the Arun from the boarding boat off Spurn in the extremely poor conditions was a difficult and dangerous task, but once the crew were aboard

Coxswain Bevan headed out at full speed. The blizzard reduced visibility and a thick layer of ice stuck to the boat, having to be chipped off the radar scanner before it worked effectively. *City of Bradford IV* battled on, although concern was growing for the Wells lifeboat in the appalling conditions. However, a few minutes later the Wells lifeboatmen saw one of the ships and reached *Savinesti* at 1.07pm. The Wells lifeboat and her crew had taken a terrible battering, with waves up to 40ft high engulfing the lifeboat. Attempts were made to get a line aboard *Savinesti* from the two vessels already standing by, but this proved impossible so the Wells lifeboat just stood by on scene awaiting the Humber boat. When *City of Bradford IV* was seven miles from the casualty, the Wells lifeboat was released to try and get back in the daylight. The wind had risen to hurricane force twelve as she set off for home. She reached the coast at 6.15pm and, covering the last seven miles in two hours, fought through the mountainous seas to reach harbour safely.

Back at sea, further attempts were made to get a line aboard *Savinesti*, but without success so, with the other vessels and the Humber lifeboat escorting her, the casualty headed slowly north, making four knots at best. Shortly after midnight, as the snow finally eased and the wind dropped to force nine, *Savinesti* and the other ships, then about five miles north of the Dowsing lightvessel, turned to head for the Humber. They eventually entered the river at 3am, and *City of Bradford IV* returned to her moorings at 4.25am after over fifteen hours at sea. For this long and extremely difficult and demanding service, undertaken in the worst weather for many years, Coxswain David Cox of Wells was awarded the silver medal, with medal service certificates going to the rest of the Wells crew. Coxswain Bevan was awarded the bronze medal, and medal service certificates were presented to the rest of the Humber crew. The winter of 1978-79 had seen some of the worst weather in living memory along the east coast, and the feats of the Humber lifeboatmen, led by Coxswain Brian Bevan, in their 54ft Arun lifeboat were as considerable as any performed in the history of the lifeboat service, and the Arun was proving to be possibly the best lifeboat type ever designed by the RNLI.

Another gold medal-winning service was undertaken in 1981 when *Sir William Arnold*, the second Arun to be built and which had served at St Peter Port since 1973, was launched to help the motor vessel *Bonita*, which was in distress in the English Channel, listing forty degrees to starboard and had thirty-six people on board, including women and children on 13 December. *Sir William Arnold* slipped her moorings at 2pm under the command of Coxswain Michael Scales and set out at full speed into the southerly storm force ten, gusting to hurricane force twelve while driving snow and sea spray had reduced visibility to 200 yards. Course was set north through Little Russel Channel, but the radar was blanked out by heavy snow showers and the boat was

Medal services undertaken in Arun lifeboats

Year	Date	Station	Arun	Awards	Casualty
1975	15 July	St Peter Port	52-02	Bronze medals to Coxswain John Petit and Emergency Mechanic John Robilliard	Motor vessel Point Law
1976	14 Oct	Weymouth	54-04	Silver medal to Coxswain Victor Pitman	Yacht Latifa
1976	6 Dec	Torbay	54-03	Gold medal to Coxswain Keith Bower, bronze medals to Mechanic Stephen Bower, Assistant Mechanic William Hunkin, and crew members Richard Brown, Nicholas Davies, John Drew and Michael Mills	Motor vessel Lyrma
1977	11 Nov	St Peter Port	52-02	Bronze medal to Coxswain John Petit	Sloop yacht Canopus
1978	19 Feb	Torbay	54-03	Bronze medal to Coxswain George Dyer	Pilot cutter Leslie H
1978	2 Dec	Torbay	54-03	Bronze medal to Coxswain Arthur Curnow	Trawler Fairway
1978	30 Dec	Humber	54-07	Silver medal to Superintendent Coxswain Brian Bevan	Coaster Diana V
1978	4 Jan	St Peter Port	52-02	Bronze medal to Coxswain John Petit	Motor vessel Cantonad
1979	14 Feb	Humber	54-07	Gold medal to Superintendent Coxswain Brian Bevan, bronze medals to Second Coxswain Dennis Bailey, Mechanic Bill Sayers, Asst Mechanic Ronald Sayers, and crew Dennis Bailey jnr, Peter Jordan, Sydney Rollinson, Michael Storey	Motor vessel Revi
1979	15 Feb	Humber	54-07	Bronze medal to Superintendent Coxswain Brian Bevan	Freighter Savinesti
1981	2 Oct	Campbeltown	52-12	Silver medal to Coxswain Alexander Gilchrist	Trawler Erlo Hills
1981	13 Dec	St Peter Port	52-02	Gold medal to Coxswain Michael Scales, bronze medals to Second Coxswain Peter Bougourd, Mechanic Robert Vowles, Assistant Mechanic Alan Martel and crew Peter Bisson, John Bougourd, Richard Hamon, John Webster	Motor vessel Bonita
1981	13 Dec	Humber	54-07	Bronze medal to Superintendent Coxswain Brian Bevan	Coaster Harry Mitchell
1982	21 Sep	Lerwick	52-10	Bronze medal to Coxswain Hewitt Clark	Yacht Hermes of Lune
1984	24 Jan	St Peter Port	52-02	Bronze medal to Coxswain Michael Scales	Freighter Radiant Med
1985	11 Aug	St Peter Port	52-02	Bronze medal to Second Coxswain Peter Bisson	Yacht Matam II
1986	15 Apr	Tynemouth	52-13	Silver medal to Coxswain Captain John Hogg	Fishing vessel la Morlaye
1987	16 Oct	Weymouth	54-04	Bronze medal to Coxswain Derek Sargent	Catamaran Sunbeam Chaser
1988	13 Sep	Kirkwall	52-39	Bronze medal to Coxswain Captain William Sinclair	Cement carrier BC Mercurius
1988	27 Oct	Mallaig	52-21	Bronze medal to Coxswain Thomas Ralston	Fishing vessel Galilean
1989	13 Jan	Lerwick	52-10	Bronze medal to Coxswain Hewitt Clark	Fishing vessel Boy Andrew
1989	28 Oct	Yarmouth	52-34	Bronze medal to Coxswain David Kennett	Cargo vessel Al Kwather I
1992	29 Aug	St Peter Port	52-02	Silver medal to Coxswain Peter Bisson	Yacht Sena Sioria
1993	17 Jan	Lerwick	52-10	Bronze medal to Coxswain Hewitt Clark	Motor fishing vessel Ardency
1993	17 Nov	Lerwick	52-10	Bronze medal to Second Coxswain William Clark	Trawler Borodinskoye Polye
1994	6 Oct	Penlee	52-24	Bronze medal to Coxswain Neil Brockman	Crabber Julian Paul
1994	31 Oct	Lerwick	52-10	Silver medal to Coxswain Hewitt Clark	Factory ship Pionersk

navigated by Decca. Near Brehon Tower, *Sir William Arnold* broached for the first time but full speed was resumed immediately. About three-quarters of an hour later, the lifeboat broached again and broached six more times during passage to the casualty, but full speed was maintained throughout.

The lifeboat arrived on scene at 4.30pm with the wind still force eleven and seas of fifteen metres to contend with. Two helicopters and four large vessels were near the casualty, and four people had been lifted off by a Sea King helicopter from RNAS Culdrose, but all subsequent attempts at rescue had failed. *Bonita* was listing forty-five degrees to starboard and rolling heavily, with her rails and stanchions in the water, and seas sweeping her decks. St Peter Port lifeboat was manoeuvred round the stern and Coxswain Scales instructed the casualty's crew to make their way to the stern, the only place from which the lifeboat could effect a rescue. One man fell as he moved into position, breaking his leg, and all his colleagues could do was lash him to the hatch to stop him being swept overboard.

At the stern Coxswain Scales found that his lifeboat was rising and falling 50ft, bringing her level with *Bonita's* after deck on each crest, and the bottom edge of the casualty's rudder in the troughs. He could not lie alongside for any length of time, and in order to get the lifeboat in position to rescue *Bonita's* crew had to make repeated runs in to the vessel.

On the first such run, three men jumped to the lifeboat but their timing was poor and they fell 25ft to the deck. One man struck the lifeboat's stanchions and deckhouse, and was injured so badly that he later died. As soon as the three survivors were aboard, the lifeboat was swept into the debris around the ship, but, by using only his starboard engine which was furthest from the flotsam, Coxswain Scales brought the lifeboat clear without fouling her propellers. Scales then approached head on to the transom, with the lifeboat crew down the port side secured by their lifelines. While the lifeboat was held under helm and engines, Second Coxswain Peter Bougourd threw a heaving line to two women, who attached it around themselves and jumped into the sea. At this point, the lifeboat came gently astern on her engines, so the survivors could be recovered aboard the lifeboat's lower side deck aft and then taken to the deckhouse where Mechanic Robert Vowles attended to them.

The next approaches were similar to this and resulted in five people being rescued. Twice survivors let go of the line when they were in the water and then swam clear of the casualty so the lifeboat crew could pick them up. One man, without a life jacket, fell from the stern of *Bonita* while the lifeboat was recovering the next survivor and was swept down the starboard side of the motor vessel. Having recovered the first survivor, the lifeboat searched for the man who had fallen, but he appeared to be dead so Coxswain Scales returned to take off more survivors using the heaving line. Some runs had to be abandoned to avoid severe damage to the lifeboat and during one violent astern manoeuvre first one engine, then the other, failed. Although both were restarted quickly, the bow of the lifeboat was trapped under the chine of *Bonita's* transom until the restarted engines pulled the rescue boat astern and clear.

The lifeboat made about fifty runs in to the transom, ten of which were to take off one man who could not hold onto the heaving line. He eventually wrapped the line around his hands and was then pulled into the sea. Having recovered sixteen survivors, Coxswain Scales took the lifeboat upwind of *Bonita* to give the crew a respite, in good view of the casualty. In the freezing temperature and heavy spray, circulation was restored, aching muscles were eased and lifelines were adjusted before the lifeboat again approached *Bonita*. During the respite, a helicopter made several attempted rescues and succeeded in lifting off one man. The lifeboat crew continued to recover survivors using the heaving line, although both rescuers and rescued were frequently engulfed by heavy seas. One man was not breathing when he was lifted aboard, but crew member John Webster took action to expel water from his mouth before taking him to the wheelhouse, where Mechanic Vowles was helping the survivors out of wet clothes and into the heated forward and after cabins. The captain of *Bonita* was the last man to be recovered. He confirmed that only one man was left on board and, as he had a broken leg, he could not be moved to the transom.

In view of the serious condition of the severely-injured survivor on the lifeboat, Coxswain Scales decided to set course for Brixham. The RFA tanker *Olna*, acting as on-scene commander since her arrival at 5.06pm, had already informed the lifeboat that a helicopter was returning, having refuelled, and would try to lift off the one remaining man, and indeed the lifeboat crew later found out that

◄Three photos in a sequence showing the self-righting trials of 52-40 City of Plymouth at her builder's yard. All the Aruns were deliberately capsized to prove their self-righting capability. (Paul Russell)

the injured man had been rescued. Coxswain Scales asked Brixham Coastguard if Torbay lifeboat, the 54ft Arun *Edward Bridges (Civil Service and Post Office No.37)*, was still needed to assist the helicopter. The Torbay boat had left station with three additional crew, dry oilskins and provisions at 6pm to help St Peter Port lifeboat, which, at 7.54pm, began heading for Brixham. The Torbay lifeboat continued on her way, but about a mile from *Bonita* the one injured man on board was rescued by the French tug *Abeille Languedoc*. So, as she was no longer needed, the Torbay lifeboat returned to her station.

Sir William Arnold, with her tired crew and survivors, had a rough journey north. A few minutes after leaving the scene, she fell into a deep trough while steaming into the force ten to eleven winds, and speed had to be reduced to prevent further injury to survivors. She arrived at Brixham at 11.13pm, where she was met by members of the Torbay station. Coxswain Scales kept the survivors on board until blankets had been provided to ease the shock of emerging into the bitter cold. The exhausted St Peter Port crew spent the night at Brixham, returning to the Channel Islands the following day, with the Arun having suffered only minimal damage. The injured survivor died two days after the rescue, and *Bonita* sank the day after the rescue.

For this service the gold medal for conspicuous gallantry was awarded to Coxswain Scales of St Peter Port lifeboat and bronze medals were awarded to each of the crew: Second Coxswain Peter Bougourd, Mechanic Robert Vowles, Assistant Mechanic Alan Martel and crew members John Webster, John Bougourd, Peter Bisson and Richard Hamon. A framed letter of thanks signed by the Duke of Atholl, chairman of the Institution, was sent to Captain Claude Jouin, master of the French tug *Abeille Languedoc*, and letters of appreciation signed by Rear Admiral W. J. Graham, director of the Institution, were sent to the commanding officers of RNAS Portland and Culdrose and to the masters of RFA *Olna* and *Charlottenburg*. Letters signed by Rear Admiral Graham were also sent to Captain B. J. Anderson, Torbay station honorary secretary, expressing appreciation to Coxswain Arthur Curnow and his crew for the help given to the crew of St Peter Port lifeboat and the survivors of *Bonita*.

Sir William Arnold was involved in a number of remarkable medal-winning services during her time at St Peter Port, while another Arun, *Soldian* (ON.1057), undertook a similar number of medal-winning rescues during her time at Lerwick.

▶ The Donaghadee lifeboat 52-33 City of Belfast on exercise. (Rick Tomlinson, by courtesy of the RNLI)

No fewer than four bronze medals were awarded to her coxswains during this time, as well as one silver medal for a rescue in the early hours of 31 October 1994 when *Soldian* went to aid of the 10,074-tonne *Pionersk*, which, with 155 people on board, had run aground at Trebister Ness, about three miles south of Lerwick, in gale force eight winds, gusting to storm force ten. In fifteen minutes the lifeboat, under the command of Coxswain Hewitt Clarke, was alongside *Pionersk*, which was yawing violently in a heavy swell. Four survivors were quickly recovered from a ladder, but that became so badly damaged that it could not be used.

So the lifeboat was taken round the stern of the casualty and, with the storm force ten winds causing a strong swell making the boat very difficult to handle, had to be manoeuvred into position with less than 20ft of sea to the cliffs. Coxswain Clark had to make between seventy and eighty approaches to recover the other sixty-three men from the stricken vessel, as only one man at a time could be taken off. The lifeboat crew had to cling on to the rails as the lifeboat rolled while, at the same time, help the frightened Russian crew down onto the heaving deck of the lifeboat. At times the lifeboat crew had to crouch below the level of the rails to avoid being crushed between the two vessels. The rescuers' task was made more difficult when the casualty's engine room was flooded and the engines and generators stopped, leaving the lifeboat crew working in total darkness.

At 2.48am the lifeboat advised the Coastguard that sixty-seven survivors were on board and that she would return to Lerwick to land them. By 3.10am the lifeboat was alongside her berth and, once the survivors had been landed, she returned to the casualty to stand by while the helicopter evacuated the remaining crew on board. At 4.29am the Coastguard asked the lifeboat to pick up the remaining four crew, including the captain, as the helicopter, which had made eight lifts to take off eighty-four men, was refuelling at Lerwick. But the helicopter returned and lifted them off before *Soldian* was needed, so the lifeboat stood by until all the crew were accounted for and then returned to station.

▲ 52ft Arun 52-32 Keith Anderson which served at Newhaven and Hartlepool. (By courtesy of the RNLI)

▲ Two Aruns together off Longhope, June 2004: 52-43 The Queen Mother (on right) and 52-28 Sir Max Aitken II are put through their paces as the former replaces the latter at the station. (Nicholas Leach)

During this outstanding service the Arun lifeboat had saved no fewer than sixty-four lives while operating in the most appalling conditions, and Magnus Shearer, the Lerwick station honorary secretary, commented: 'The coxswain and crew were called on to make a superhuman effort in rescuing sixty-seven crew members from a vessel in what amounts to impossible conditions. The fact that no lives were lost or injuries sustained sometimes makes it seem easy. But the seamanship, consummate skill and boat handling ability of Coxswain Hewitt Clark is second to none. To go in and take the lifeboat alongside the vessel where there was absolutely no margin for error is a skill in itself, but to do it in the conditions which prevailed that night and in total darkness is beyond belief – to do so over seventy times without loss of life or injury is surely nothing short of a miracle. I have never seen the coxswain and crew so physically and mentally shattered after a service and they really did give of their all.' For his outstanding seamanship and courage, Coxswain/Mechanic Hewitt Clark was awarded the silver medal by the RNLI, and the Thanks of the Institution on Vellum was accorded to Second Coxswain/Assistant Mechanic Peter Thomson and crew members Ian Fraser, Iain Tulloch, Robert Wiseman and Richard Simpson.

While this was probably the most difficult service undertaken by *Soldian* at Lerwick, it was just one of numerous award-winning rescues carried out by the Lerwick lifeboatmen in the Arun. Indeed, by the mid-1990s Coxswain Clark had been awarded no fewer than three bronze medals for rescues in *Soldian*. The first of these was on 21 September 1982 when the lifeboat saved three crew from the yacht *Hermes* in a hurricane, rough seas and torrential rain. As well as the bronze medal awarded to Coxswain Clark, the Thanks of the Institution on Vellum was accorded to Assistant Mechanic Andrew Leask and Emergency Mechanic Ian Newlands for taking a line ashore in the lifeboat's inflatable Y boat.

Another medal-winning service was carried out on 13 January 1989, when

Soldian was launched to the fishing vessel *Boy Andrew*, which had run aground near Bressey lighthouse. The vessel had been pulled clear by another fishing vessel, but had been holed and, in deteriorating conditions, quickly sank. Just as she was going down, Coxswain/Mechanic Hewitt Clark took the lifeboat in at full speed to save the three fishermen still on board. For his outstanding seamanship another bronze medal was awarded to Coxswain Clark and the Thanks of the Institution on Vellum was accorded to crew members Robert Wiseman and Iain Tulloch, who had manned the lifeboat's inflatable Y boat.

Four years later, on 13 January 1993, *Soldian* was again involved in an outstanding service, going to the fishing vessel *Ardency,* which had broken down in horrendous seas and winds gusting to ninety knots. A tow rope was rigged by the lifeboat crew, and pumps were lowered to the casualty by the Coastguard helicopter, but the passage back to Lerwick could only be undertaken at about two knots. The tow line parted at one point, and it took forty-five minutes before it was reconnected, during which time heavy seas repeatedly swept both lifeboat and casualty making the rescuers' work particularly difficult. Lerwick harbour was reached at 8.15am, by when the lifeboat had been on service for the best part of ten hours. In recognition of his great courage and fine leadership, a further bronze medal was awarded to Coxswain Clark, his third such award from the RNLI.

Later the same year, on 17 November, yet another outstanding service was performed by the Lerwick crew in *Soldian*. This time, with joint Second Coxswain William Clark in command, the lifeboat went to the fish factory ship *Borodinskoye Polye*, which had run aground in the northern approaches to Lerwick in exceptionally heavy seas and winds gusting to force ten. In saving thirty-seven people, the lifeboat was taken alongside the casualty thirty-five times. During the rescue operation, the lifeboat was rising and falling twenty feet in the heavy swell, and getting the boat into position to save the men who had descended a ladder involved a considerable feat of seamanship. For this excellent service, the bronze medal was awarded to Second Coxswain Clark, who also received the Maud Smith Award for the bravest act of lifesaving in 1993. The RNLI's Thanks on Vellum was accorded to Joint Second Coxswain/Assistant Mechanic Peter Thomson, Emergency Mechanic Ian Fraser and crew members Robert Wiseman, Richie Simpson and Theo Nicholson.

While these dramatic medal-winning rescues represent the most notable of the services carried out by the RNLI's Arun lifeboats, the boats were also involved in more mundane rescues and many achieved fine records of service. The second of the class, 52-02 *Sir William Arnold*, completed over 500 effective services during her time at St Peter Port, including the medal rescues, while in just ten years on station in Galway Bay covering the Aran Islands, 52-36 *Roy and Barbara Harding* launched more than 300 times on service. The Weymouth boat, 54-04 *Tony Vandervell*, the first of the GRP-hulled boats, performed almost 600 services. The boats' complete service records can be found in the individual entries, with details of the stations they served.

Arun construction ceased in 1990 when the final boat of the class, 52-46 *The Duke of Atholl*, was completed and entered the Relief Fleet. A total of forty-six Aruns had been completed,

▼ The sad sight of Rosslare Harbour's 52ft Arun 52-26 St Brendan after she had been badly damaged by the Stena Line ferry Koningin Beatrix on 9 September 2001. The force of the collision destroyed the steel framework of the pen and caused extensive damage to the lifeboat, but she remained afloat and was able to make her way, under her own power, to the nearby marina at Kilmore Quay for inspection. She was subsequently taken out of servcie and scrapped. (By courtesy of Rosslare Harbour RNLI)

▲ SAR512 is one of a number of Aruns built for the Hellenic Coast Guard, for service around the Mediterranean in Greek waters.

of which nine had been built for the Relief Fleet. By then the RNLI was producing fast designs of slipway and carriage launched lifeboats, respectively the Tyne and Mersey classes, and plans for new designs to replace the Aruns and Waveneys were being formulated. The intention was to develop two types of boat which could reach speeds of twenty-five knots, and by the early 1990s the prototypes of these boats were undertaking trials. The larger of the two was the 17m Severn, which ended up replacing the majority of Aruns, although at a number of stations the smaller 14m Trents took over, and at one station, Longhope, the Arun was replaced by a 16m Tamar, the design developed during the early twenty-first century primarily as a slipway-launched lifeboat. The last few Aruns to leave RNLI service were sold in 2007 with the final Arun to be disposed of, 52-43 *The Queen Mother*, going to the Montevideo Pilots Association in 2009.

Such was the excellence of the Arun design that several lifeboat societies around the world have used it. In 1988 a steel-hulled 52ft Arun was built by the Canadian Coast Guard, the success of which led to the building of further Aruns in aluminium for service in Canada, and a total of ten were in service by the mid-1990s. The first of the class, *Bickerton*, was built by Halmatic at Havant in 1989 and had a Kevlar-construction hull, while the rest were built in Canada of aluminium. The boats were similar to the RNLI's Aruns, and measured 16.25m by 5.18m by 1.25m. They were initially designated as Large Search-and-Rescue Lifeboats Type 310, but this was later changed to Multi-Task High Endurance Lifeboats. They were usually manned by a crew of four, which was made up of two officers and two non-officers.

The type was also used in Greek waters, with ten boats moulded and fitted out by Halmatic at Northam for the Greek Coastguard. The Greek boats were slightly larger than the British Aruns, with a displacement of thirty-four tons and a length of 18m, or 59ft, and a beam of 17ft 6in. They were powered by twin Caterpillar 3408BTA diesels totalling 1,000bhp, and carried a range of electronic equipment including Furano Loren C90 radio navaid, Anschutz gyrocompass, and an

Aruns built for Canadian CG

Name	In service	Builder
Bickerton	Aug 1989	Halmatic, Havant
Spindrift	Oct 1993	Georgetown Shipyard, Prince Edward Island
Spray	Sep 1994	Industries Raymond, Sept Îles, Quebec
S. Jackman	Oct 1995	Industries Raymond, Sept Îles, Quebec
Spume	Oct 1994	Industries Raymond, Sept Îles, Quebec
W. G. George	Sep 1995	Industries Raymond, Sept Îles, Quebec
Cap-aux-Meules	Oct 1996	Hike Metal Products, Wheatly, Ontario
Clark's Harbour	Sep 1996	Hike Metal Products, Wheatly, Ontario
Sambro	Jan 1997	Hike Metal Products, Wheatly, Ontario
Westport	May 1997	Hike Metal Products, Wheatly, Ontario

integrated communications system on the bridge. The boats all entered service in 1997-98 and remain in use in the Mediterranean, numbered LS-511 to LS-520.

Meanwhile, as the Aruns were gradually replaced by the RNLI during the 1990s, they were taken out of service and sold, with many going to overseas rescue organisations to continue their life-saving careers as some had relatively few years of life-saving service. They therefore represented excellent value for the China Rescue & Salvage Bureau, which bought ten, while fifteen were sold to ICE-SAR in Iceland, where they form the basis of that country's all-weather lifeboat fleet. Unfortunately one boat, 52-16 *Richard Evans*, was lost while being transported north to Iceland when she broke free from the deck of the motor vessel *Skaftarfell* and was washed overboard. The remains of the boat were found three days later on a rocky beach in Iceland with the only recognisable item the Y class inflatable, which was holed. The engines showed where the boat stranded and debris was scattered over a 300 metre radius. However, despite this tragedy, ICE-SAR continued to operate Aruns with some success, and deployed a total of thirteen of the boats. Aruns were also sold by the RNLI to the rescue services in Finland, Faroe Islands, Chile and Australia.

◄ The last 52ft Arun in RNLI service was 52-43 The Queen Mother, pictured here at the RNLI Depot, Poole in January 2009 prior to her sale. (By courtesy of the RNLI)

A number of Aruns were sold out of service to private buyers in the UK, and they have been used for a variety of purposes. The first two boats of the class, 52-01 *Arun* and 52-02 *Sir William Arnold*, ended up with owners basing them in Scotland and Ireland respectively, where they are maintained in near original condition. The third boat, and the last of the wooden Aruns, is the only one that has been preserved and is on display, kept at the Historic Dockyard at Chatham as part of the Historic Lifeboats collection, maintained by a group of willing and dedicated volunteers. And so the Aruns live on, both in the UK in various roles, and in countries around the world, where their award-winning design continues to give good service saving lives at sea.

Part Two
The Arun class boat by boat

52-21 The Davina and Charles Matthews Hunter. (RNLI)

Op No	ON	Name	Built	Left service	Page no
52-01	1018	Arun	1971	1997	38
52-02	1025	Sir William Arnold	1973	1998	40
54-03	1037	Edward Bridges (Civil Service & Post Office No.37)	1974	1994	42
54-04	1049	Tony Vandervell	1976	1999	44
54-05	1050	B. P. Forties	1976	1998	46
54-06	1051	The Gough-Ritchie	1976	1998	48
54-07	1052	City of Bradford IV	1977	1998	50
52-08	1053	Joy and John Wade	1977	2002	52
52-09	1056	Spirit of Tayside	1978	1999	54
52-10	1057	Soldian	1978	2002	56
52-11	1058	Elizabeth Ann	1979	2002	58
52-12	1059	Walter and Margaret Couper	1979	2001	60
52-13	1061	George and Olive Turner	1979	2000	62
52-14	1062	Edith Emilie	1980	1999	64
52-15	1067	Hyman Winstone	1980	2003	66
52-16	1070	Richard Evans (Civil Service No.39)	1981	2003	68
52-17	1071	Sir Max Aitken	1981	2003	70
52-18	1073	Robert Edgar	1981	2003	72
52-19	1076	Marie Winstone	1981	2002	74
52-20	1077	Duchess of Kent	1981	2003	76
52-21	1078	Davina and Charles Matthews Hunter	1982	2003	78
52-22	1081	Ralph and Bonella Farrant	1982	2005	80
52-23	1082	Margaret Frances Love	1982	2005	82
52-24	1085	Mabel Alice	1983	2004	84
52-25	1086	A. J. R. and L. G. Uridge	1983	2003	86
52-26	1092	St Brendan	1983	2001	88
52-27	1093	Charles Brown	1983	2005	90
52-28	1098	Sir Max Aitken II	1984	2005	92
52-29	1099	Joseph Rothwell Sykes and Hilda M.	1983	2002	94
52-030	1100	Snolda	1984	2007	96
52-31	1103	Newsbuoy	1984	2005	98
52-32	1106	Keith Anderson	1985	2006	100
52-33	1107	City of Belfast	1985	2005	102
52-34	1108	Margaret Russell Fraser	1986	2004	104
52-35	1113	City of Dublin	1986	2004	106
52-36	1118	Roy and Barbara Harding	1986	2004	108
52-37	1123	Kenneth Thelwall	1987	2005	110
52-38	1134	City of Glasgow III	1987	2005	112
52-39	1135	Mickie Salvesen	1988	2006	114
52-40	1136	City of Plymouth	1987	2004	116
52-41	1143	Ann Lewis Fraser	1988	2005	118
52-42	1144	Murray Lornie	1988	2005	120
52-43	1149	The Queen Mother	1989	2009	122
52-44	1150	Hibernia	1988	2007	124
52-45	1159	Mabel Williams	1990	2007	126
52-46	1160	Duke of Atholl	1990	2007	128

52-01

Arun

OFFICIAL NUMBER
1018

YEAR BUILT
1971

BUILDER
William Osborne Ltd,
Littlehampton

YARD NO
WO 22/1018

WEIGHT
25 tons 5 cwt

COST
£99,110

DONOR
Gift from Birds Eye Foods,
Miss Alice Johnston, and
legacies of Miss E. H. Eastland,
Miss M. Harrison, Miss F. J. Hart
and Miss V. E. Young.

STATIONS
St Peter Port (Guernsey)
15 Oct 1972 – May 1973
(25/13)
Barry Dock
7 Jun 1974 – May 1997
(331/75)

DISPOSAL
Sold out of service Oct 1997
to the engineering firm LADCO
of Dundee

Although the first Arun to be built was something of an experimental design, she entered service and had a full life-saving career for the best part of a quarter of a century. Named *Arun*, she was the first of only three Aruns to have wooden hulls, and was completed by William Osborne Ltd at their Arun Shipyard, Littlehampton, in 1971.

As the first of a new and revolutionary lifeboat design, she was used for trials and evaluation for over a year, going on a tour of lifeboat stations in Britain and Ireland. In May 1971 she was taken by a delegation from the RNLI to Malmø, Sweden, for an International Conference of voluntary lifeboat organisations organised by the Swedish Lifeboat Service. During her voyage from Dover to Scandinavia, *Arun* visited ports in the Netherlands, Germany, Denmark and Norway.

Arun spent much of 1971 touring lifeboat stations around the British Isles, including a visit to London in June 1971, when she was moored near Lambeth Bridge. During this tour, she was in Scrabster for the naming of the new Thurso 48ft 6in Solent lifeboat *The Three Sisters* on 11 August, having been installed as station lifeboat at Kirkwall for a few months. In total, on passage evaluation trials she undertook ten launches, five in 1971 and five in 1972, and saved two lives.

Arun was formally named at a ceremony on 23 September 1972 at Littlehampton, where she had been built, by Mrs Ralph Farrant having been formally handed over to the RNLI by Mr K. J. B. Webb, chairman of Birds Eye Foods Ltd. She had been funded by Birds Eye Foods through the 'Help to launch a lifeboat' appeal, together with gifts from Miss Alice Johnston and legacies left by E. H. Eastland, Miss M. Harrison, Miss F. J. Hart and Miss V. E. Young.

After the successful completion of her evaluation trials, she was sent to St Peter Port as station lifeboat. She arrived at Guernsey on 15 October 1972 and was placed on service there after a dedication ceremony at which William T. Bishop, a member of the Committee of Management, addressed the crowd. She spent more than a year at St Peter Port, launching on service twenty-five times, before being replaced by the second Arun, *Sir William Arnold*, in November 1973. She spent the next six months acting as a relief lifeboat at St Peter Port, until being reallocated to Barry Dock in May 1974.

Before taking up her station duties, *Arun* was sent to Ocean Fleet's boatyard at Birkenhead for overhaul, and then went to Barry Dock in early June 1974. She served for more than twenty-years at the South Wales station covering the Bristol Channel, during which time she launched 331 times on service and saved seventy-five lives.

When built, *Arun* was equipped with twin 375hp Caterpillar D336TA eight-cylinder engines. On 26 June 1991 she was taken to the Falmouth Boat Co yard in Cornwall, where she was given a complete overhaul and re-engined with twin 485hp Caterpillar 3208TA diesel engines with which she reached a top speed of just over fifteen knots. The work was finished by April 1992 and, after a series of trials, she left Falmouth in June and returned to Barry Dock.

In May 1997 *Arun* was replaced by another 52ft Arun lifeboat, *Margaret Frances Love*, and was then taken to the RNLI Depot at Poole to be sold. In October 1997 she was purchased by the engineering firm LADCO and renamed *Arun Adventurer*. She has operated from Dundee Docks as a publicity boat for more than a decade, and is occasionally moored at Broughty Ferry and also visits Arbroath.

▲ Barry Dock: at moorings when on station, August 1988. (Nicholas Leach)

▼ Barry Dock: leaving harbour on exercise, March 1997. (Nicholas Leach)

Sir William Arnold

OFFICIAL NUMBER
1025

YEAR BUILT
1973

BUILDER
William Osborne Ltd,
Littlehampton

YARD NO
WO 93/1025

WEIGHT
28 tons 13 cwt

COST
£132,095

DONOR
Special Local Appeal.

STATIONS
St Peter Port (Guernsey)
Dec 1973 – Jun 1997
(503/224)

DISPOSAL
Sold out of service on 24 Feb
1998 to Mr T. Gill and Mr C. P.
McGuinness

Sir William Arnold, the second Arun, was significantly different from the prototype. Although her hull was the same shape as that of *Arun,* and it was built from wood, it had a cutaway freeboard amidships to make it easier to recover survivors from the water. The second boat had a much modified wheelhouse arrangement, although the flying bridge was situated aft as it had been on the prototype, *Arun.*

After completion by William Osborne at Littlehampton, *Sir William Arnold* was sent to Guernsey in July 1973 on evaluation trials and during that month launched twice on service, saving six lives. After a week of crew training during November 1973, she was placed on station as the St Peter Port lifeboat on 8 November, replacing the prototype *Arun.*

Sir William Arnold was funded from a special local appeal in Guernsey, which raised £55,000, and as a result was named after the Bailiff of Guernsey who had been heavily involved in the appeal. The boat's official naming took place on 23 May 1974 when HRH Duchess of Kent, visiting Guernsey for the first time, christened the boat, which was handed over to the Guernsey branch by Commander F. R. H. Swann, chairman of the RNLI.

Sir William Arnold served at Guernsey for almost a quarter of a century, launched over 500 times on service, and was involved in some notable rescues. The first of these took place on 11 November 1977 when she launched to the yacht *Canopus,* of France, which was stranded on rocks in gale force winds. Getting the lifeboat alongside the yacht in the heavy seas proved to be extremely difficult, and Coxswain John Petit had to make four approaches to save the four people on board. For this service Coxswain Petit was awarded the bronze medal, and

the Thanks on Vellum was accorded to Deputy Coxswain Peter Bougourd and crew member Robert Harman.

The outstanding service of *Sir William Arnold's* career came on 13 December 1981 when she launched to the Ecuadorian cargo vessel *Bonita,* which was listing heavily in severe weather almost forty miles north of Guernsey. A full description of this rescue can be found in Part One.

Another medal-winning rescue took place on 24 January 1984 when the lifeboat went to the cargo vessel *Radiant Med,* of Liberia. In storm force winds and very high seas, *Sir William Arnold* was thrown on to her beam ends during the rescue, but despite this the nine crew from the coaster were saved from their life raft. The Bronze medal was awarded to Coxswain Michael Scales and the Thanks on Vellum to Mechanic Robert Vowles following this service.

Another outstanding service took place on 11 August 1985 to the yacht *Matam II.* Three people were rescued and the yacht, which was anchored below cliffs at Corbiere, was saved in a force eight to nine southerly gale and heavy breaking seas. The bronze medal was awarded to Acting Coxswain Peter Bisson, and the Thanks on Vellum to Assistant Mechanic Alan Martel and crew member John Guille.

Sir William Arnold continued to give good service throughout the remainder of the decade and well into the 1990s. She was replaced by a 17m Severn class lifeboat in June 1997, and on 15 June was taken to the RNLI Depot at Poole for disposal, and on 24 February 1998 she was sold out of service to Mr T. Gill and Mr C. P. McGuinness, of Didsbury, Manchester, who renamed her *Our Lady* and kept her unaltered as a pleasure boat at Fleetwood. She later went to Liverpool and then Cork.

▲ St Peter Port: at moorings in the harbour, October 1996. (Nicholas Leach)

▼ On exercise off Guernsey. (Brian Green)

Edward Bridges (C. S. & P. O. No.37)

OFFICIAL NUMBER
1037

YEAR BUILT
1974

BUILDER
William Osborne Ltd,
Littlehampton

YARD NO
WO 700

WEIGHT
30 tons 8 cwt

COST
£162,383

DONOR
Civil Service and Post Office
Lifeboat Fund; named after
Head of the Civil Service

STATIONS
Torbay
Aug 1975 – 16 Apr 1994
(456/285)

DISPOSAL
Withdrawn from service 1994;
Oct 1996 went to Chatham
Historic Dockyard for display

As the RNLI further developed the Arun, the third example of the class had her stern lengthened by 2ft, which made the boat 54ft overall. She was the first of seven 54ft Aruns to be constructed. The superstructure arrangement on the third boat was also modified, with the flying bridge moved forward to give better visibility to the helmsman, while the cutaway freeboard in the hull introduced in the second of the class was retained.

This boat was the third and last Arun to be built of wood. She was completed by William Osborne at Littlehampton in October 1974, and then taken on evaluation trials around the country. During October 1974, while on evaluation trials between Kirkwall and Peterhead, a passage service took place to a sick man on an uninhabited island. She was then allocated to the Torbay station, based out of Brixham.

Funded by the Civil Service and Post Office Lifeboat Fund, she was named *Edward Bridges (Civil Service and Post Office No.37)* after the late Baron Bridges, who had a long career in the Civil Service. As the Torbay lifeboat, she was named at Brixham in the afternoon of 17 June 1975 by HRH The Duke of Kent after the Duchess of Kent had named the new Plymouth Waveney lifeboat *Thomas Forehead and Mary Rowse II* in the morning of the same day. The Torbay boat was formally handed over to the RNLI by Lord Bridges, son of Baron Bridges.

After an evaluation and trial period, *Edward Bridges* was placed on station at Torbay on 16 April 1975 and went on to serve the station for almost two decades, operating from a mooring in Brixham harbour, where she became a well-known sight to locals and visitors. She had an outstanding record of service in Devon, and is credited with saving almost 300 lives during her career.

The most notable service in which she was involved took place on 6 December 1976, when she saved ten people from the cargo vessel *Lyrma*, of Panama, for which Acting Coxswain Keith Bower was awarded the gold medal. An account of this service can be found in Part One.

Another noteworthy service by *Edward Bridges* took place on 19 February 1978, when she launched at 12.33pm to the pilot cutter *Leslie H*. The lifeboat was knocked down at one point by a giant wave, estimated at more than 30ft in height, and a crew member was swept overboard, but was immediately recovered. Three men were then taken off the cutter, which later sank. The Bronze medal was awarded to Coxswain George Dyer for this service.

Towards the end of the same year, on 2 December 1978, another challenging service was undertaken when six crew were saved from the trawler *Fairway* in storm force winds and heavy seas. The trawler had broken down and was drifting ashore about eight miles south of Lyme Regis. Coxswain Arthur Curnow skillfully manoeuvred the lifeboat alongside the casualty twice to effect a rescue. For his skill and leadership, the Bronze medal was awarded to Coxswain Curnow.

In April 1994 *Edward Bridges* left Torbay to go for a survey at Berthon Boat Co at Lymington. This revealed severe deterioration in the boat's hull and decking and, as a result, the lifeboat was withdrawn from operational service immediately, and options for her disposal were considered. She remained at Berthon Boat Co's yard for more than a year, until a decision had been taken about her disposal. Then, in October 1995, she was taken to Chatham Historic Dockyard for permanent display out of the water as part of the Lifeboat Collection, along with several other historic lifeboats.

▲ Bringing to safety a broken down
yacht. (By courtesy of the RNLI)

▼ Torbay: returning to Brixham harbour.
(By courtesy of the RNLI)

Tony Vandervell

OFFICIAL NUMBER
1049

YEAR BUILT
1976

BUILDER
Halmatic Ltd hull, fit out
by William Osborne Ltd,
Littlehampton

YARD NO
WO 1250

WEIGHT
31 tons 16 cwt

COST
£143,824

DONOR
The Vandervell Foundation

STATIONS
Weymouth
Mar 1976 – Jun 1999
(598/359)

DISPOSAL
Sold out of service on 5 May
1999 to the Finland Lifeboat
Service

The fourth Arun was the first lifeboat to be built of glass reinforced plastic (GRP). The hull was moulded in GRP by Halmatic at Havant between January and June 1974, and it was then fitted out by William Osborne at Littlehampton. The boat was completed in early July 1975 and between 9 and 14 July was taken to various lifeboat stations around the coast on trials. On 12 July, while on passage from Fishguard to Holyhead, she undertook a passage service to the cabin cruiser *Jane*.

She returned to her builder's yard after the passage, before embarking on further trials for the rest of 1975 that lasted until March 1976. During her trials she travelled a total of 6,000 miles, and proved to be capable of maintaining her full speed in very severe conditions. Following her final forty-hour trials, she was taken to her new station at Weymouth, travelling from Littlehampton via an overnight call at St Peter Port. She arrived at Weymouth on 15 March 1976 and, after three days of crew training, was placed on station on 19 March.

Named *Tony Vandervell*, the new boat was provided through a gift from The Vandervell Foundation, of Cheapside, London, which had been set up by the late Mr G. A. 'Tony' Vandervell, a noted industrialist. She was formally named at a ceremony at Weymouth on 17 September 1976 by Commander F. R. H. Swann, CBE, a Vice-President of the Institution, after being handed over to the RNLI by Mr J. L. Reed, a trustee of the Foundation.

During a twenty-three-year career at Weymouth, *Tony Vandervell* undertook almost 600 services, which was a remarkable record of service. She was also involved in some fine rescues, the first of which took place the year she become operational.

On 14 October 1976 she went to the yacht *Latifa,* of Southampton, which had been badly damaged in storm force winds and severe sea conditions. With the wind worsening to hurricane force, and after being thrown on her beam ends several times, the Arun lifeboat reached the yacht. At the third attempt a line was passed across, and in the treacherous conditions the tow was completed. The yacht and her eight crew were rescued. For this service a silver medal was awarded to Acting Coxswain Victor Pitman for his leadership and determination on only his second trip in command.

As well as this service, *Tony Vandervell* was used in three other noteworthy rescues when her crew gained the RNLI's Thanks inscribed on Vellum. On 24 September 1978 she saved two people from the yacht *Sartorius*, which had gone aground about nine miles from Weymouth, for which Second Coxswain Victor Pitman was accorded the Thanks on Vellum. On 11 August 1985 she went to the yacht *Vagrant Gypsy* which was in difficulties in a strong south-westerly gale and confused seas. The lifeboat took off three people, after which a towline was successfully passed across. This gained Coxswain Pitman another Thanks on Vellum award.

In June 1999 *Tony Vandervell* was replaced at Weymouth by another Arun, *Robert Edgar*, and was taken to the RNLI Depot at Poole having already been sold to the Finnish Lifeboat Service. She arrived at Poole on 11 June and was almost immediately handed over to her new owners. Four days later she sailed to Finland to continue her life-saving career. She was renamed PR *Mac Elliot* at a ceremony in Finland on 14 August 1999 and was stationed at Porkkala, a small harbour twenty miles west of Helsinki.

▲ Weymouth: moored on station,
October 1994. (Nicholas Leach)

▼ Weymouth: returning to harbour after a
service, 1996. (Andrew Cooke)

54-05

B. P. Forties

OFFICIAL NUMBER
1050

YEAR BUILT
1976

BUILDER
Halmatic Ltd, Havant

YARD NO
4665

WEIGHT
31 tons 16 cwt

COST
£158,455

DONOR
British Petroleum Co Ltd and
the students of Aberdeen
University

STATIONS
Aberdeen
3 Jun 1976 – Aug 1998
(112/11)

DISPOSAL
Sold out of service on 27
Oct 1998 to ICE-SAR, the
National Lifesaving Association
of Iceland

After the first glass reinforced plastic-hulled Arun was sent for service on England's south coast, in 1975 the second GRP boat was allocated to Aberdeen, a busy port on Scotland's east coast. The station had been served by Barnett class lifeboats, the largest of the RNLI's displacement boats, and was an ideal station for the more technologically advanced Arun.

The new lifeboat was named *B. P. Forties* having been provided by The British Petroleum Co Ltd, of Britannic House, London, as well as the students of Aberdeen University who raised £7,000 to cover the cost of the lifeboat's electronic equipment. The boat was fitted out by Halmatic at Havant during the first part of 1976, and arrived at Aberdeen on 1 June 1976 to be escorted into harbour by a flotilla of vessels including the station's former lifeboat *Ramsay Dyce* and the D class inflatable inshore lifeboat.

B. P. Forties was named on 8 September 1976 at Aberdeen's Regent Quay. Chairman of the branch, Mr R. M. Addison, welcomed guests and supporters to the occasion. David Steel, Chairman of BP, which had made a gift under deed of covenant of £100,000 towards the new lifeboat, handed her over to the RNLI.

Mr I. Barclay, representing the students of Aberdeen, presented a cheque which, together with the lifeboat, was accepted on behalf of the Institution by Sir Charles McGrigor, BT, Convener of the Scottish Lifeboat Council and a member of the Committee of Management. He in turn delivered the boat into the care of the Aberdeen branch and she was accepted by the honorary secretary, Captain Brian Atkinson. There followed a service of dedication led by the Rev James S. Wood and the lifeboat was named by Mrs David Steel.

B. P. Forties served at Aberdeen for twenty-two years and performed more than 100 services during that time. One of the more unusual rescues in which she was involved took place on 31 July 1980 after a British Airways S-61N helicopter, which was returning from an oil rig, ditched in the sea seventeen miles off Aberdeen. The lifeboat made best speed for the scene, and then towed the helicopter into the harbour after all the people on board it had been evacuated safely.

During her time at Aberdeen, *B. P. Forties* visited the neighbouring harbour of Stonehaven a number of times. On 29 July 1984 she attended a quayside church service there to commemorate the RNLI's 160th anniversary, and on 20 June 1997, she participated in a Sea Survival Conference organised by the Maritime Rescue Institute.

After being replaced at Aberdeen in August 1998, *B. P. Forties* left the station the following month and was taken to Buckie Boatyard, where she remained until November 1998. Having been sold out of service to ICE-SAR, the Icelandic lifeboat service, she left Buckie on 11 November 1998 and was sailed north to her new home. During the long passage, she stopped for fuel at Kirkwall, the Orkney capital, before proceeding overnight to Thorshavn on the Faroe Islands and then on to Eidj in the North Faroes.

On 15 November 1998 she left the Faroes and made for Höfn, on Iceland's south eastern coast. After a passage of thirty hours, during which the boat covered 330 miles, she reached Höfn. From there she went to the Vestmannaeyjar Islands and the port of Heimaey, and arrived at Grindavík on 17 November. She was renamed *Oddur V. Gislason* and began work as a lifeboat for ICE-SAR based out of Grindavík, serving that station until 2007.

▲ On trials prior to coming to Aberdeen.
(By courtesy of the RNLI)

▼ Aberdeen: moored on station, July
1994. (Nicholas Leach)

The Gough-Ritchie

OFFICIAL NUMBER
1051

YEAR BUILT
1976

BUILDER
Halmatic Ltd hull, fit out
by William Osborne Ltd,
Littlehampton

YARD NO
WO 1255

WEIGHT
31 tons 12 cwt

COST
£171,270

DONOR
Gift of Mrs Ann A. Ritchie,
Baldrine, Isle of Man

STATIONS
Port St Mary
Sep 1976 – May 1998
(166/63)

DISPOSAL
Sold out of service on
16 Jul 1998 to the Cuerpo
de Volantarios de los Botes
Salvavidas de Valparaiso, Chile

The sixth Arun lifeboat was allocated to Port St Mary, on the Isle of Man, where she replaced a 46ft 9in Watson motor lifeboat. She was fitted out by William Osborne during 1976, and was ready for service by August that year. Between 19 and 28 August 1976 she was at Poole, and completed her forty-hour trials at the end of the month.

During the first week of September 1976 she sailed to the Isle of Man, and, on 9 September 1976, was placed on station at Port St Mary, a station she served with distinction for almost twenty-two years. She was funded by a gift from Man resident Mrs Ann Ritchie, who had previously provided the Ramsey lifeboat *James Ball Ritchie*, and was named *The Gough-Ritchie*, as Gough was the donor's maiden name.

The Gough-Ritchie was named at a ceremony held on 21 July 1977 at the Inner Harbour, Port St Mary. In front of a large crowd, Mrs Ritchie formally handed over the lifeboat to the RNLI, and she was accepted by Major-General Ralph Farrant, RNLI Chairman, who handed her in turn to John Hudson, Honorary Secretary of the station. After the service of dedication, Mrs Ritchie named the lifeboat. Among those present at the ceremony were J. A. McLachlan, designer of the Arun hull.

The most notable rescue in which *The Gough-Ritchie* was involved took place on 17 May 1981, after the yacht *Melfort* went aground on rocks at Derbyhaven in gale force south-easterly winds. The lifeboat put out at 9.10am and, once on scene, the small inflatable Y boat was used to get close to the casualty. It then stood by as one of the yacht's four crew was rescued by breeches buoy. When the yacht began to break up, the Y boat was immediately taken alongside. But

while the lifeboatmen freed one man from the wreckage, the breaking waves pushed the inflatable away, throwing the casualty and a lifeboatman into the water, and capsizing the dinghy. The two lifeboatmen were swept down to the breakwater, but nothing could be seen of the yachtsman.

Another of the yacht's crew was pulled aboard the lifeboat by a line thrown to him from *The Gough-Ritchie*, and the body of the man who had disappeared was later recovered by helicopter. Following this service, The Thanks of the Institution on Vellum were accorded to Coxswain/Mechanic Norman Quillin and crew members Eric Quillin and William Halsall, who had manned the Y boat.

In May 1998 *The Gough-Ritchie* was replaced by a new 14m Trent named *Gough-Ritchie II*. The Arun was then taken to the RNLI Depot at Poole, leaving Port St Mary for the last time on 26 May 1998 and travelling south via overnight stops at Fishguard, Newlyn and Brixham. She was put up for sale, and shown to purchasers from overseas lifeboat services, being sold on 16 July 1998 for £55,000 to the Cuerpo de Volantarios de los Botes Salvavidas de Valparaiso of Chile.

With the sale complete, the boat was taken to Liverpool for shipping, travelling there via Salcombe, Newlyn, Fishguard and Holyhead. On 11 September 1998 she arrived at Liverpool, entered Gladstone Lock and was lifted aboard the Hamburg Sud container ship *Veruda*, which left on 14 September 1998 and took the boat to South America free of charge. She was unloaded at San Antonio, forty miles south of Valparaiso, on 17 October. She then sailed north to Valparaiso where, having been renamed *Capitan Eduardo Simpson Roth*, she resumed her role as a lifeboat.

▲ Port St Mary: Leaving harbour after her naming ceremony,
21 July 1977. (By courtesy of Port St Mary RNLI)

▼ Port St Mary: moored on station,
May 1995. (Nicholas Leach)

54-07

City of Bradford IV

OFFICIAL NUMBER
1052

YEAR BUILT
1977

BUILDER
Halmatic Ltd, Havant

YARD NO
WR4908

WEIGHT
32 tons 8 cwt

COST
£163,453

DONOR
City of Bradford Appeal,
Sheffield Lifeboat Fund and the
International Transport Workers'
Federation

STATIONS
Humber
Mar 1977 – Aug 1987
(416/106)
Thurso
26 Mar 1988 – Mar 1989
(12/2)
Ballyglass
17 Oct 1989 – Aug 1990 (9/0)
Tobermory
7 Feb 1991 – Jul 1998
(186/24)

DISPOSAL
Sold out of service on 22 Oct
1998 to M. Rice, Riverside
Developments Ltd

The important station at the Humber, manned by a full-time crew based at Spurn Point, was allocated an Arun class lifeboat in 1975 once it was realised that a permanent mooring was available in the river. The Arun destined for the Humber, the last of the 54ft versions to be built, was fitted out by Halmatic, at Havant, during 1976.

City of Bradford IV was named on 10 September 1977 at a ceremony organised jointly by the Hull and Bradford Branches. The Arun was the fourth Humber lifeboat named *City of Bradford*, and her cost was met by the City's Lord Mayor's appeal 1974-75 supported by the Bradford and District Branch, several other branches, the Sheffield Lifeboat Fund, the International Transport Workers' Federation, various gifts and legacies.

While a relief lifeboat and crew gave temporary cover at Spurn Point, *City of Bradford IV* was brought by her full-time crew to King George Dock, at Kingston-upon-Hull, with the wives and children following by road. Sir Basil Parkes, OBE, President of the Hull Branch, opened proceedings and Clifford Kershaw, Chairman of Bradford Branch, presented the lifeboat to the RNLI. Councillor T. E. Hall, Lord Mayor of Bradford 1974-75 and patron of the appeal committee, formally named the lifeboat.

City of Bradford IV had arrived at the Humber in March 1977 and served the station for a decade. She was involved in a series of remarkable rescues during the winter of 1978-79 that earned Coxswain Brian Bevan and his crew nationwide fame, with Bevan receiving gold, silver and bronze medals.

The first of Coxswain Bevan's three medals, a silver, was awarded after the rescue of six people from the Dutch coaster *Diana V*, which was in difficulty

seventy-four miles east of Spurn Point on 30 December 1978. The ship's cargo had shifted in the severe weather and the lifeboat had to battle through storm force winds and freezing temperatures which caused the sea water to freeze on the deck.

Coxswain Bevan received a gold medal for a rescue carried out on 14 February 1979, to the Panamanian motor ship *Revi*, which is described in detail in Part One. And just over twenty-four hours after she had returned to station from this rescue, Humber lifeboat again put out, and her crew spent seventeen hours at sea in storm force winds and blizzards. She joined the Wells 37ft Oakley lifeboat *Ernest Tom Neathercoat* in helping the cargo ship *Savinesti*, with twenty-eight people on board, which was in danger of running aground. Coxswain Bevan received a bronze medal and Wells' Coxswain David Cox a silver medal for their efforts during this service.

After being replaced at Humber in August 1987, *City of Bradford IV* was reallocated to Thurso, where she became the first lifeboat at that station to go afloat, being based in the harbour at Scrabster. After a year there, she become the first lifeboat at Ballyglass, a newly opened station on the west coast of Ireland. She was used as the station's lifeboat during a twelve-month period of evaluation and crew training.

In 1991 *City of Bradford IV* returned to Scotland and spent the last seven years of her career at Tobermory on Mull. She left there in July 1998 and, after a week on relief at Fishguard, arrived at the RNLI Depot in Poole on 9 August 1998 ready for disposal. Static display at Portsmouth Festival of the Sea weekend in late August followed, she was placed on the sale list on 1 September and sold out of service in October 1998.

▲ Humber: On exercise off Spurn Point.
(By courtesy of the RNLI)

▼ Tobermory: moored on station,
August 1997. (Nicholas Leach)

Joy and John Wade

OFFICIAL NUMBER
1053

YEAR BUILT
1977

BUILDER
Halmatic Ltd hull, fit out
by William Osborne Ltd,
Littlehampton

YARD NO
WO 1565

WEIGHT
32 tons 14 cwt

COST
£186,877

DONOR
The Wade Foundation, Isle of
Wight Lifeboat Appeal, together
with eight legacies

STATIONS
Yarmouth
19 Jul 1977 – Jan 2001
(677/258)
Relief Fleet
Jan 2001 – Aug 2001 (3/0)

DISPOSAL
Sold out of service in Jun
2002 to the National Lifesaving
Association of Iceland

The eighth Arun to be built, *Joy and John Wade*, had a flying bridge and superstructure arrangement that became the standard for the subsequent Arun build programme. The flying bridge was forward on the wheelhouse, as with the 54ft Aruns, but the stern was squared so she was 52ft overall, and subsequent Aruns were all built to this design.

The boat was largely funded by The Wade Foundation, through E. J. Wade of Wymering House, Sandy Lane, Lyndhurst, together with the Yarmouth IOW Lifeboat Appeal, which provided the combined funds to cover the building costs of £187,000, along with various legacies. She was named *Joy and John Wade* after the main donors.

Before she took up duties at her Isle of Wight station, *Joy and John Wade* represented the RNLI at HM The Queen's Silver Jubilee Fleet Review on 28 and 29 June 1977, one of three offshore lifeboats, while two Atlantic 21 ILBs were involved. The Yarmouth crew gave three cheers for Her Majesty as the Royal yacht *Britannia* passed during the parade.

Following the Fleet Review, *Joy and John Wade* was placed on station at Yarmouth on 19 July 1977 and her naming ceremony took place on 24 July, when HRH The Duke of Kent, President of the RNLI, was on hand to name the boat. The harbour at Yarmouth was packed with yachts and small boats, and Lymington's Atlantic 21 B-519 was also present.

During the night before her naming, the lifeboat had performed her first services. She had been called out three times, spending ten hours at sea attending two yachts and investigating distress flares off Atherfield Ledge. The crew were delighted with the boat's performance and her speed in the rough weather.

During the ceremony John Wade and his wife handed over the lifeboat to the RNLI on behalf of the Foundation, and Major General R. A. Pigot, who had launched the Appeal, was also present. After the Duke had performed the formal naming, the lifeboat took the invited guests out into the waters of the Solent for a short trip.

In more than two decades of service at Yarmouth, *Joy and John Wade* undertook almost 700 service launches, making her one of the busiest of the Aruns. One of the most noteworthy rescues she performed took place on 3 July 1978 when she launched under Coxswain David Kennett in gale force winds and rough seas to the yacht *Turpina*. Using the Y boat, crew members Stuart Pimm and Richard Downes transferred a line from the casualty to the lifeboat, which was towed to safety. The two crew were awarded framed letters of thanks signed by the RNLI chairman for their efforts.

Another test for the Arun lifeboat and her crew came on 16 October 1987, when Britain was hit by the worst storms in 200 years. *Joy and John Wade* put out in the worst conditions Coxswain David Kennett had ever experienced to stand by the coaster *Union Mars*, which had suffered steering failure three miles off St Catherine's Point. Because the coaster's crew managed to repair the vessel's steering, the lifeboat was not needed, but a letter of thanks was sent to the station from Brian Miles, the RNLI's Chief of Operations.

After being replaced in January 2001, *Joy and John Wade* spent a few months in the Relief Fleet before being sold out of service to ICE-SAR, the National Lifesaving Association of Iceland in June 2002. She was renamed *Björg* and stationed at Rif, a small harbour on Iceland's west coast.

▲ Yarmouth: on exercise off the Isle of Wight in the mid-1980s. (Andrew Cooke)

▼ Yarmouth: moored in the harbour, August 1999. (Nicholas Leach)

Spirit of Tayside

OFFICIAL NUMBER
1056

YEAR BUILT
1978

BUILDER
Halmatic Ltd, Havant

YARD NO
WR5172

WEIGHT
34 tons

COST
£231,729

DONOR
Donations to the Broughty Ferry
Lifeboat Appeal, together with
several legacies

STATIONS
Broughty Ferry
6 May 1978 – Feb 1999
(123/1)

DISPOSAL
Sold out of service on 30 May
1999 to the Royal Volunteer
Coastal Patrol, Australia

Spirit of Tayside was allocated to the Broughty Ferry station near Dundee, where she replaced the 47ft Watson motor lifeboat *The Robert*. The Watson had been slipway-launched from a boathouse into the river, so the new Arun was the station's first lifeboat to be moored afloat. The moorings in the fast-flowing Tay were reached by an inflatable boarding boat, which was kept in the boathouse.

Unusually, the new lifeboat was fitted out by Halmatic at Havant, the company that also moulded her GRP hull, and she was completed by the spring of 1978. After a series of trials out of the RNLI's Depot at Poole in April 1978, training for the crew took place early the following month, and on 6 May 1978 she was placed on service at Broughty Ferry after she had completed her passage north. She was funded by the Broughty Ferry Lifeboat Appeal, led by Branch President Ian Low, which raised £226,000 towards her cost between 1975 and 1977 through a number of fund-raising events which were held in the area.

Spirit of Tayside was formally named on 17 July 1978 at Broughty Ferry Harbour by HRH The Duke of Kent, President of the Institution, after what was a somewhat unusual handing-over ceremony. Ian Low, president of Dundee branch, who handed over the boat to Sir Charles McGrigor, Bt, convener of the Scottish Lifeboat Council, then delivered her straight back again into the care of Dundee branch for use at Broughty Ferry. She was accepted by honorary secretary, Captain R. W. Forbes.

The service of dedication was conducted by the Rev J. U. Cameron and the Rev T. P. Robertson. Then the Duke, following in the footsteps of his mother Princess Marina, named the lifeboat. After he had performed the naming, he went aboard *Spirit of Tayside* for a short trip.

The most dramatic service in which *Spirit of Tayside* was involved took place on 24 December 1978 when she went to the cargo vessel *Fendyke* in gale force eight to nine winds. During the incident the lifeboat was knocked down by two huge waves, the second of which was between thirty and thirty-five feet high. One crewman was knocked unconscious while in the toilet during the knock downs, Second Coxswain Hugh Scott broke his ankle and Coxswain John Jack sustained injuries to his leg. The lifeboat received superficial damage and she was forced to make for the shelter of Leith after a very difficult operation.

After almost twenty-one years of service at Broughty Ferry, *Spirit of Tayside* was replaced by another 52ft Arun, *Joseph Rothwell Sykes and Hilda M*, in February 1999 and placed on the sale list. She was then taken to the RNLI Depot at Poole, travelling from Tayside via overnight stops at Amble, Scarborough, Gorleston, Ramsgate and Shoreham.

She was stored at Poole until July 1999, by when she had been sold for further service with the Australian Royal Volunteer Coastal Patrol. Between 11 and 14 May she was taken to Alderney on a familiarisation trip with Australian representatives on board, calling at Salcombe and Weymouth on the way back.

Once the sale had been finalised, on 31 July 1999 *Spirit of Tayside* left Poole and was taken to Tilbury Docks via Newhaven and Sheerness for shipping to Australia on board a container ship. She left Tilbury on 2 August 1999, and upon arrival in Australia was renamed *PV Daniel Thain* and deployed by the Port Stephens Division of the RVCP.

▲ Broughty Ferry: on exercise in the river Tay. (By courtesy of the RNLI)

▼ Broughty Ferry: moored in the river Tay, July 1994. (Nicholas Leach)

Soldian

OFFICIAL NUMBER
1057

YEAR BUILT
1978

BUILDER
Halmatic Ltd hull, fit out
by William Osborne Ltd,
Littlehampton

YARD NO
WO 1850

WEIGHT
32 tons 2 cwt

COST
£225,452

DONOR
Lerwick Lifeboat Appeal,
including Brent and Ninian
Pipeline Consortium Chevron
Petroleum (UK) Ltd, The
Aberdeen Students' Charities
Campaign together with various
legacies from Miss Blyth,
Miss Dickinson, Mr Gray, Miss
Halcrow and Mrs Rae

STATIONS
Lerwick
23 Aug 1978 – Jun 1997
(245/260)
Relief Fleet
Jun 1997 – Jan 1998 (1/0)
Achill
10 Jan 1998 – Apr 1999 (6/3)
Relief Fleet
5 May 1999 – Dec 2001
(10/0)

DISPOSAL
Sold out of service in
Mar 2002 to ICE-SAR, the
National Lifesaving Association
of Iceland

The Lerwick lifeboat station, one of two in Shetland, was allocated an Arun class lifeboat in 1977. The boat was fitted out by William Osborne at Littlehampton during the first six months of 1978 and at the start of July 1978 was delivered to the RNLI's Depot at Poole. She had been funded through the Lerwick Lifeboat Appeal including members of the Brent and Ninian Pipeline Consortium, Chevron Petroleum (UK) Ltd, the Aberdeen Students Charities Campaign, and legacies from Miss Blyth, Miss Dickinson, Mr Gray, Miss Halcrow and Mrs Rae, and was named *Soldian*.

After a month at Poole, during which training by the Lerwick crew had taken place, she left on 27 July 1978 and reached Dover the same day, before crossing the Channel to Belgium the following day and calling at Nieuwport and Blankenberge. She headed north on 30 July and made for Gorleston, where she stayed until 3 August with engine problems. With these resolved, she left for Whitby, staying there on 3 August before going to Dundee on 4 August, Kirkwall on 5 August, and the last leg to Lerwick on 6 August.

The new lifeboat was named at Lerwick on 12 September 1978 by HRH The Duke of Kent, president of the RNLI, who was visiting Shetland for the first time for the occasion. More than 2,500 people had gathered at the pier for the ceremony, which was also attended by the Norwegian lifeboat *Skomvaer II* and her crew. The Arun was handed over to the RNLI by Lady Steel on behalf of the Oil Consortium and all the other donors. She was accepted by Major-General Ralph Farrant, RNLI chairman, who in turn passed her into the care of Lerwick honorary secretary, Magnus Shearer.

Soldian served at Lerwick for the best part of two decades and gained a fine record of service, being involved in several medal-winning rescues. The first of these rescues took place in 1982 when Coxswain/Mechanic Hewitt Clark was awarded a bronze medal for the rescue of three crew and the yacht *Hermes of Lune*, which was dragging her anchor near Out Skerries in a south-westerly hurricane, rough seas and rain on 21 September.

In 1989 Coxswain/Mechanic Clark was awarded another Bronze medal for rescuing three crew members from the fishing vessel *Boy Andrew*, which was aground on rocks at Trebister Ness on 13 January. Just over four years later on 17 January 1993, *Soldian* went to the aid of the fishing vessel *Ardency* in horrendous conditions with winds gusting to ninety knots, and saved the vessel's crew of six, a service for which Coxswain Clark was awarded his third bronze medal.

In October 1994 Coxswain Hewitt Clark received a silver medal for a rescue which is fully described in Part One, and four days later Soldian was called upon again. On 4 November, in gale force winds, she safely brought in the fishing vessel *Achilles*, for which Thanks on Vellum was accorded to Acting Coxswain William Clark.

In June 1997 *Soldian* was replaced at Lerwick by a new 17m Severn class lifeboat, and after a year in the Relief Fleet she served at Achill, a new station on the west coast of Ireland. After fifteen months there, she was replaced by a new lifeboat and served as a Relief lifeboat again until December 2001, when she was placed on the sale list. She was sold out of service in 2002 to ICE-SAR, the Icelandic Lifeboat Association and left Poole on 24 March 2002 to go to Immingham, from where she was transported to Iceland. She was stationed at Reykjavik and renamed *Asgrimur S. Björnsson*.

▲ Lerwick: winching exercise with HM Coastguard's Sikorsky
helicopter 'Oscar Charlie'. (By courtesy of the RNLI)

▼ Achill: moored in Achill Sound,
April 1999. (Nicholas Leach)

Elizabeth Ann

OFFICIAL NUMBER
1058

YEAR BUILT
1979

BUILDER
Halmatic Ltd hull, fit out
by William Osborne Ltd,
Littlehampton

YARD NO
WO 1945

WEIGHT
32 tons 1 cwt

COST
£299,737

DONOR
Gift of Sir John Slater
Foundation and the Sir
Kirby Laing Foundation, the
Cornish Lifeboat Appeal, and
various other gifts and legacies

STATIONS
Falmouth
19 Jun 1979 – 1997 (249/52)
Relief Fleet
7 Feb 1998 – Dec 2001 (67/3)

DISPOSAL
Sold out of service in Jun 2002
to the Royal Volunteer Coastal
Patrol, Australia

The first Arun lifeboat to serve in Cornwall was allocated to Falmouth, where the natural harbour provided an excellent sheltered mooring. After fitting out by William Osborne's yard at Littlehampton, the new lifeboat was sent to Falmouth in June 1979 and placed on service on 19 June. She had been funded from the gift of Sir John Slater Foundation and the Sir Kirby Laing Foundation, supplemented by the Cornish Lifeboat Appeal and other legacies and gifts including the proceeds of special efforts by Falmouth branch, and was named *Elizabeth Ann*.

Before her formal naming ceremony, *Elizabeth Ann* was one of many lifeboats which assisted the numerous yachts caught out by severe weather during the infamous Fastnet Race of August 1979. She was tasked to search an area west of the Isles of Scilly and, in extremely heavy seas, checked out a number of yachts before taking in tow the yacht *Big Shadow* that had nine crew on board and suffered a broken rudder. She also towed the abandoned yacht *Golden Apple of the Sun* to Newlyn and checked out two further vessels in the Falmouth area before returning to station, having been away for over sixty-two hours.

Elizabeth Ann was named on 10 June 1980 at the Customs House Quay, Falmouth. Philip Fox, president of the station branch, oversaw proceedings as the new Arun was presented to the RNLI by the Right Honourable the Viscount Falmouth, representing the various donors. The lifeboat was accepted by Surgeon Captain F. W. Baskerville, a vice-president of the RNLI, who gave her into the care of Falmouth branch and honorary secretary Captain D. G. Banks.

Following a service of dedication conducted by the Right Rev Graham D. Leonard, Lord Bishop of Truro, assisted by the Rev Peter Boyd and the Rev David Roberts, Mrs Joyce Hulme, a relative of Mrs Elizabeth Ann Slater, performed the naming ceremony. In command for the last time before his retirement, Coxswain Arthur 'Toby' West, demonstrated the manoeuvring qualities of the new Arun in the inner harbour before the guests boarded for a short trip.

Elizabeth Ann's most notable service came on 15 February 1985 when she escorted the sinking French trawler *St Simeon*, which was in difficulty thirteen miles south of the Lizard, a service for which Coxswain Vivian Pentecost was accorded the Thanks of the Institution on Vellum. Just over ten years later, on 26 November 1995, *Elizabeth Ann* saved two crew from the catamaran *Cloud Nine*, which resulted in the Thanks on Vellum being accorded to Coxswain Alan Barnes and crew member Peter Wood.

Elizabeth Ann served at Falmouth for eighteen years, during which time she saved more than fifty lives. After being replaced by one of the first 17m Severn lifeboats in March 1997, she served in the Relief Fleet for the last five years of her career, starting with short stints in 1997 at Torbay, Newhaven and Harwich. She later went to St Mary's (1998) and Penlee (1999), and then to several stations in both Ireland and Scotland until being withdrawn from service in 2001.

Elizabeth Ann was sold in June 2002 to the Royal Volunteer Coastal Patrol in New South Wales, Australia and was shipped there by a P&O Nedlloyd container ship. Renamed *P&O Nedlloyd Encounter,* she initially served as Sydney Harbour lifeboat, based at The Spit, Mosman, in Sydney's Middle Harbour, before becoming the Ulladulla lifeboat.

▲ Falmouth: heading out of Falmouth on exercise. (Paul Richards)

▼ Falmouth: on exercise off the Cornish coast. (Rick Tomlinson, by courtesy of the RNLI)

52-12

Walter and Margaret Couper

OFFICIAL NUMBER
1059

YEAR BUILT
1979

BUILDER
Halmatic Ltd, Havant

YARD NO
WR5845

WEIGHT
32 tons

COST
£302,748

DONOR
Legacy of Miss Margaret G.
Couper, in memory of her
father and mother

STATIONS
Campbeltown
14 Sep 1979 – May 1999
(274/130)
Relief Fleet
May 1999 – May 2001
(13/1)

DISPOSAL
Sold out of service on 1 May
2001 to the Finland Lifeboat
Service

The first Arun to serve on the west coast of Scotland was *Walter and Margaret Couper*. She was allocated to Campbeltown in 1978 where she was to replace a 52ft Barnett lifeboat which had been on station since 1953. As the Campbeltown lifeboat had been kept afloat since the arrival of the first motor lifeboat, the station was ideally suited to a new Arun. To improve boarding arrangements, however, a new dedicated pontoon facility was put in place alongside the Old Quay, especially for the Arun.

After being placed on station on 14 September 1979, the new boat was named at Campbeltown's inner harbour on 12 July 1980. The service of dedication was conducted by the Rev J. R. H. Cormack, Minister of the Lowland Church, and Lady Cunninghame Graham by Lesley Gilchrist, daughter of the coxswain, there was a welcome for everyone from Rear Admiral R. W. Mayo, chairman of the branch, who also introduced the principal guests among whom was Sir Charles McGrigor, Convener of the Scottish Lifeboat Council.

Admiral Sir Angus Cunninghame Graham, a vice-president of the RNLI, accepted the new lifeboat on behalf of the Institution from Mrs Thomas Couper. The lifeboat was funded almost entirely from a bequest from the late Miss M. G. Couper and was dedicated to her parents, Walter and Margaret. He then handed the lifeboat over to Mr J. P. McWhirter, honorary secretary, who accepted her on behalf of the Campbeltown branch. After a vote of thanks proposed by Mrs A. D. Wallace, president of Campbeltown ladies' guild, Lady Cunninghame Graham christened the new lifeboat.

Walter and Margaret Couper had a tremendous record of service at Campbeltown and served with distinction for almost two decades. She was involved in a number of fine rescues, the most notable of which took place on 2 October 1981 after the trawler *Erlo Hills* went ashore off Rathling Island. A full account of this service, for which Coxswain Alexander Gilchrist was awarded the silver medal, can be found in Part One.

As well as this medal-winning rescue, *Walter and Margaret Couper* was involved another fine service. On 29 March 1995 the lifeboat was used to rescue the skipper, Dick Gannon, of the work boat *Gille Brighde,* who was trapped in the wheelhouse after the vessel had capsized. Various attempts were made to get to him, but not until one of the boat's windows smashed was it possible to reach him. Two lifeboat crew in the water grabbed him and the lifeboat's winch was used to lift the vessel's bows out of the water, enabling other crew members to drag the survivor to safety. Coxswain Jim McPhee was accorded the Thanks Inscribed on Vellum for this service.

After a fine career at Campbeltown, *Walter and Margaret Couper* was replaced in May 1999 by a new 17m Severn class lifeboat and she was used as a Relief lifeboat for a year. She spent much of that time at her old station covering for the new Severn class lifeboat, including a short stint in July and August 1999 while the Severn went up to Glasgow to attend the Tall Ships event at Greenock.

She served on Relief duty at Fenit and Torbay in 2000, and then went to the RNLI Depot at Poole for storage in May 2000 prior to being sold out of service to the Finnish Lifeboat Service. She left Poole on 19 May 2001 and was taken to Finland, where she served as a lifeboat at Turku before being transferred to the port of Hanko in 2004 and renamed *PR Russarö.*

▲ On trials ready to go on station, with the Y boat launch davit prominent. (By courtesy of the RNLI)

▼ Campbeltown: on exercise in Campbeltown Loch, July 1995. (Nicholas Leach)

George and Olive Turner

OFFICIAL NUMBER
1061

YEAR BUILT
1979

BUILDER
Halmatic Ltd hull, fit out
by William Osborne Ltd,
Littlehampton

YARD NO
WO 2020

WEIGHT
31 tons 16 cwt

COST
£302,286

DONOR
Legacy from Mrs O. B. Turner,
the Sir James Knott Trust, the
Tyneside Lifeboat Appeal, and
other gifts and legacies

STATIONS
Tynemouth
22 Feb 1980 – Oct 1999
(285/58)
Relief Fleet
21 Oct 1999 – Aug 2000 (1/0)

DISPOSAL
Sold out of service on 18 Aug
2000 to ICE-SAR, the National
Lifesaving Association of
Iceland

In 1979 a new Arun was allocated to the Tynemouth station, which covered the busy river Tyne, where a suitable berth was available at North Shields Fish Quay. Having been built at Halmatic, the boat was fitted out during 1978-9 by William Osborne and undertook her trials in August 1979. After a week of crew training and a passage north, she arrived at Tynemouth on 22 February 1980 and was placed on station six days later. Almost half the cost of the new lifeboat was provided by a legacy from Mrs O. B. Turner with the rest coming from a combination of four other legacies, a donation from the Sir James Knott Trust, the Tyneside Lifeboat Appeal, and various other gifts.

In recognition of the main donor, the new lifeboat was named *George and Olive Turner*. Her naming ceremony was held at the Fish Quay, North Shields, on 28 June 1980 and one of the clergy taking part in the service of dedication was the Rev E. B. Greathead, a descendant of Henry Greathead, builder of the first purpose-designed lifeboat, while another descendant, Mrs Greathead from Conisborough Ladies Guild, was also present.

The lifeboat was presented to the RNLI on behalf of the donors by Mr P. R. Easton and Mr J. Briggs, a nephew of the late Mr and Mrs Turner. The Duke of Northumberland, Treasurer of the Institution and a vice-president, formally accepted *George and Olive Turner*, and delivered her to the Tynemouth station. She was accepted by Honorary Secretary Ken Middlemiss and the naming was performed by the Duchess of Northumberland.

During almost two decades of service at Tynemouth *George and Olive Turner* gained a fine record of service, launching almost 300 times on service.

Her most notable rescue took place on 15 April 1986 after the 60ft fishing vessel *La Morlaye* got into difficulty in a force eight south-easterly gale. The vessel's nets had fouled her propeller, but, when being towed by another fishing vessel, the tow broke when the vessels were just north of the entrance to the Tyne. *La Morlaye* went aground and was lying inside breaking surf with 20ft waves crashing over her.

The lifeboat had to operate in darkness and only a few hundred yards from the beach. In the difficult conditions, Coxswain John Hogg made three attempts to tow the casualty clear, but without success. He then decided that there was no alternative but to risk taking the lifeboat alongside. Despite the difficult conditions, the Arun was brought close enough to the casualty for the crew of three to jump across. Following this service, the silver medal was awarded to Coxswain Hogg for saving the three crew.

In October 1999 *George and Olive Turner* was replaced at Tynemouth by a new 17m Severn class lifeboat, and then spent a year as a Relief lifeboat, serving Sunderland for a couple of weeks in November 1999. She spent most of this period at Hartlepool Marina in storage, and in May 2000 was taken south to Poole, via Grimsby, Gorleston and Dover, having been earmarked for disposal.

She was sold out of service in August 2000 to ICE-SAR, the Lifesaving Association of Iceland, and sailed from Immingham on 23 September 2000. She reached Iceland a few days later and, renamed *Gunnar Friðriksson*, was stationed at Ísafjörður. In December 2007 she was replaced at Isafjorður by another Arun, 52-46 *Duke of Atholl*, and was used as a relief boat for a year. In 2008, surplus to ICE-SAR needs, she was offered for sale.

▲ Tynemouth: moored at North Shields on station,
August 1994. (Nicholas Leach)

▼ Entering the river Tyne to return to station at
Tynemouth, July 1996. (Nicholas Leach)

52-14

Edith Emilie

OFFICIAL NUMBER
1062

YEAR BUILT
1980

BUILDER
Halmatic Ltd hull, fit out by W. A. Souter, Cowes

YARD NO
—

WEIGHT
31 tons 16 cwt

COST
£367,795

DONOR
Gift of Mrs Edith E. Currie, Brentwood, Essex

STATIONS
Relief Fleet
22 Sep 1980 – Dec 1999
(249/36)

DISPOSAL
Sold out of service on 28 Sep 1999 to A. McGreal, Osprey Aviation Ltd

▼ On trials shortly after being built. (By courtesy of the RNLI)

During the 1970s the RNLI introduced a policy of building lifeboats specifically for service in the Relief Fleet, rather than using old lifeboats that had been replaced at their stations and had a few years of service left. The first Arun to be built specifically for the Relief Fleet was *Edith Emilie*, which was fitted out on the Isle of Wight by Souter between March 1979 and May 1980.

After passing her acceptance trials on 7 May 1980, the new lifeboat was taken to the RNLI Depot at Poole to begin her career in the Relief Fleet. One of her first duties was a passage to Dunkirk, under the command of Lieut Cdr Andrew Forbes, RNLI Staff Inspector, and manned by Ramsgate crew, accompanying thirty vessels from the Association of Dunkirk Little Ships, which sailed across the Channel from Ramsgate on 30 May 1980 to commemorate the fortieth anniversary of the evacuation, spending several days in France.

Edith Emilie was christened on 22 September 1980 at the RNLI Depot, Poole, by the donor, Mrs E. E. Currie, whose family had founded a firm of timber merchants in Poole. Mrs Currie, who as a girl had often sailed with her parents from the river Hamble to

Poole, said, 'It has given me so much happiness to give this lifeboat'. Then, as she pressed the button to break the bottle of champagne, 'It gives me great pleasure to name this lifeboat after myself, *Edith Emilie*.'

Edith Emilie served in the Relief Fleet for the best part of two decades, seeing operational relief duties throughout the British Isles and Ireland. During the late 1980s she spent time relieving at various English stations, including Humber, Tynemouth, Newhaven, Dover and Weymouth. In 1989, after a survey at Robson's boatyard at South Shields, she went to the Scottish stations of Thurso, Aith and Stromness for a spell of duty.

From then, for much of the 1990s, she served as a Relief boat in Scotland, often based out of Buckie shipyard, and the following is a flavour of the duties she undertook. In 1991 she had stints at Broughty Ferry, Lerwick and Aith; in 1992 at Aith, Aberdeen and Buckie; in 1993 at Lerwick; and at Stornoway, Stromness, Aith and Kirkwall during 1994. In 1995 she spent time at Broughty Ferry and in 1996 served at Campbeltown, Lochinver, Tobermory and Mallaig. During the end of the 1990s she came to the south coast and went to St Peter Port, Weymouth, Torbay, Yarmouth, Falmouth and Newhaven during 1998 and 1999.

In 1999 *Edith Emilie* was taken out of service and placed on the sale list. She was sold out of service on 28 September 1999 to A. McGreal, of Osprey Aviation Ltd, and renamed *Ex RNLI Edith Emilie SB 1062*. She was based at Weymouth for a number of years, in use for some of the time as a safety boat off Portland harbour, until being sold again, this time to the Montrose Harbour Authority. She was used as the Montrose pilot boat having been renamed *Mare Rose*.

▲ In rough seas. (By
courtesy of the RNLI)

▼ On relief at Broughty Ferry, July
1995. (Nicholas Leach)

52-15

Hyman Winstone

OFFICIAL NUMBER
1067

YEAR BUILT
1980

BUILDER
Halmatic Ltd hull, fit out
by William Osborne Ltd,
Littlehampton

YARD NO
WO 2150

WEIGHT
31 tons 3 cwt

COST
£350,000

DONOR
Gift of Mrs Marie Winstone,
of The Gables Croft Lane
off Eccleshall Road South,
Sheffield

STATIONS
Holyhead
31 Jul 1980 – Oct 1983
(44/30)
Ballycotton
27 Apr 1985 – Mar 1998
(216/62)
Relief Fleet
Mar 1998 – Nov 1998 (0/0)
Larne
11 Nov 1998 – Aug 2000
(13/0)
Relief Fleet
Aug 2000 – 6 Jul 2002 (43/4)

DISPOSAL
Sold out of service on 30 Apr
2003 to SANAS, Madeira

Hyman Winstone was unusual in that she was built for service in Wales but ended up spending most of her career in southern Ireland. Her hull, completed by Halmatic in early 1979, was fitted out at Osborne's between January 1979 and June 1980, with crew training out of Poole during the latter part of June. She was allocated to Holyhead to replace a slipway-launched 52ft Barnett and arrived at her new station in July 1980.

Hyman Winstone was officially christened on 16 July 1980 at Holyhead's Lower Promenade by HRH The Duke of Kent, President of the Institution. The lifeboat was named in memory of the donor's husband, and Mrs Winstone, from Sheffield, said how happy she was to see so many people at the ceremony, as she delivered the boat into the care of the station.

A berth had been provided at Holyhead for the Arun, but in the long run this proved to be unsuitable, and in 1983 a 47ft Tyne class lifeboat was allocated to the station, as the Tyne could operate from the existing boathouse and slipway. So Hyman Winstone's stay at Holyhead proved somewhat short-lived, and she left in October 1983.

After a survey at Holyhead, she was stored at the RNLI Depot in Poole before going to Valentia on relief duty from August to December 1984. Between the end of her relief duty and March 1985 she underwent a survey at Crosshaven Boatyard, and then, having been reallocated to Ballycotton, came back to the RNLI Depot at Poole.

Training for Ballycotton's crew lasted until 5 April 1985, when Hyman Winstone set off for her new station, where she arrived four days later. The passage from Poole saw the boat call overnight at Weymouth, St Peter Port and Newlyn. The last port of call was

Dunmore East before Hyman Winstone made for Ballycotton on 9 April. After a further period of crew training, she was placed on station on 27 April and within two weeks had undertaken her first rescue off the Cork coast.

Hyman Winstone was rededicated at Ballycotton harbour on 8 September 1985. Amongst the huge crowd, which had come from all over County Cork, were two daughters and two grandsons of former Coxswain Patrick Sliney, who had been awarded the RNLI's gold medal for a famous rescue in 1936. The boat was blessed by the Most Rev John Ahern, Bishop of Cloyne, and the Rt Reverend Samuel Poyntz, Bishop of Cork, Cloyne and Ross.

Hyman Winstone served at Ballycotton until February 1998, when she was replaced by a new 14m Trent lifeboat, Austin Lidbury. The Arun left the station in early March 1998 and was taken to Kinsale, where she was kept stored at Kilmacsimon Boatyard before going to Holyhead Boatyard for a full refit. In October 1998 she was taken to the RNLI Depot via overnight stops at Fishguard, Newlyn, Brixham and Weymouth.

Hyman Winstone was then reallocated to the station at Larne, and she departed Poole on 24 October 1998 for her new station. She stopped at Weymouth, Falmouth, Newlyn, Kilmore Quay and Howth before reaching Bangor on 28 October. The final leg of her journey was undertaken on 29 October, when she reached Larne. She served there for less than two years before again being replaced by another new 14m Trent class lifeboat. She left Larne in August 2000 and, after a further two years in the Relief Fleet, she was taken out of service in July 2002. On 30 April 2003, she was sold to SANAS, the lifeboat service of Madeira.

▲ Ballycotton: moored in the harbour,
April 1997. (Nicholas Leach)

▼ Larne: on exercise off the Antrim
coast, May 2000. (Nicholas Leach)

52-16

Richard Evans (Civil Service No.39)

OFFICIAL NUMBER
1070

YEAR BUILT
1980

BUILDER
Halmatic Ltd hull, fit out
by William Osborne Ltd,
Littlehampton

YARD NO
WO 2250

WEIGHT
30 tons 17 cwt

COST
£272,221

DONOR
Civil Service and Post Office
Lifeboat Fund

STATIONS
Portrush
1 Mar 1981 – Jun 2000
(316/69)
Relief Fleet
Jun 2000 – Jun 2003 (0/0)

DISPOSAL
Sold out of service on 15 July
2003 to ICE-SAR Iceland but
wrecked en route to Iceland

The first 52ft Arun to be stationed in Northern Ireland was sent to Portrush in February 1981. After her hull had been moulded at Halmatic, she was fitted out by William Osborne at Littlehampton between January and November 1980, and arrived at the RNLI Depot at Poole on 26 November 1980 for final trials. Funded by the Civil Service and Post Office Lifeboat Fund, she was named *Richard Evans* after the famous former Coxswain of Moelfre lifeboat station on Anglesey, holder of two gold medals for gallantry.

Crew training took place during February 1981, and the new boat left Poole on 12 February 1981 to head for Portrush, calling at Moelfre on the way. For the last leg of her delivery trip, from Howth to Campbeltown, an exercise with the Campbeltown Arun *Walter and Margaret Couper* was held, by when Admiral Hezlet and the late Commodore Peter Kavanagh, Director of the Irish Navy, had joined the crew for the arrival at Portrush. The new lifeboat reached her station six days later and her predecessor, *Lady Scott (Civil Service No.4)*, escorted her home. After further training, *Richard Evans* was placed on station on 1 March 1981, taking up a new mooring in the harbour.

Within a couple of days of her arrival, on 27 February 1981, while crew training was still being undertaken, she was involved in a fine service after the Danish cargo vessel *Erria* ran aground in south easterly gales. *Richard Evans* slipped her moorings at 10.30pm under Coxswain Jimmy Stewart assisted by Tony Course, Divisional Inspector of Lifeboats (Ireland). Reaching the casualty three quarters of an hour later, the lifeboat stood by while three of the Danish crew were taken ashore by breeches buoy. Then, as the captain

and chief engineer had elected to remain on board *Erria*, *Richard Evans* put into Greencastle for the night in case the situation deteriorated. The two remaining Danes were finally taken off the next day by Foyle pilot boat, and the lifeboat returned to station without being further involved.

The new lifeboat was named on 27 June 1981 at Portrush with people from all over Northern Ireland present for the ceremony. Galway lifeboat, the 52ft Barnett *Frank Spiller Locke*, which was on passage, was also in attendance at the event and among the special guests were Miss Connie Henry, honorary secretary of the Civil Service and Post Office Lifeboat Fund, as well as former Coxswain Richard Evans with his wife Nancy and sons.

Sir Ronald Radford, chairman of the Civil Service and Post Office Lifeboat Fund, accompanied by Lady Radford, formally presented the lifeboat, which was handed into the care of Portrush branch honorary secretary Joe Knox. After the service of dedication, Lady Hezlet named *Richard Evans (Civil Service No.39)* with a bottle of Irish whiskey, presented by the local Bushmills distillery for the occasion, being broken over her bows.

Richard Evans served at Portrush until June 2000, launching over 300 times. She then spent three years in the Relief Fleet before being sold in July 2003. She was bought by ICE-SAR, the Icelandic lifeboat service, for duty at Raufarhöfn and left the UK as deck cargo on the coaster *Skaftarfell*. However, she was unfortunately washed overboard in severe weather during the journey north and was found completely wrecked three days later on a rocky beach in Iceland. The debris was scattered across a huge area. It was a sad end for a lifeboat which had given such good service.

▲ Portrush: on exercise off the harbour.
(Colin Watson, by courtesy of the RNLI)

▼ Portrush: moored in the harbour,
April 1997. (Nicholas Leach)

52-17

Sir Max Aitken

OFFICIAL NUMBER
1071

YEAR BUILT
1980

BUILDER
Halmatic Ltd hull, fit out by
Fairey Marine, Cowes

YARD NO
FM 707

WEIGHT
31 tons

COST
£281,953

DONOR
The Beaverbrook Foundation

STATIONS
Relief Fleet
1981 – 27 Nov 2002
(359/117)

DISPOSAL
Sold out of service on 6 Feb
2003 to Tenby Marine Services,
Marsh Road, Tenby

In 1979 the RNLI allocated another Arun for service in the Relief Fleet, the second to be built as a Relief lifeboat. The boat was fitted out during 1980 by Fairey Marine at Cowes, with the initial trials programme lasting from 21 October to 28 November 1980. After the boat's self-righting trials had been completed, the electronic equipment was fitted, and machinery and acceptance trials took place during December 1980.

In January 1981 the boat was taken to the RNLI Depot at Poole for further trials, and on 29 January went to St Peter Port for her first Relief duty. She stayed in Jersey until 15 April 1981 and then went to Cowes ready for her naming ceremony on 2 May. A donation from The Beaverbrook Foundation, of London, paid for the boat, which was named *Sir Max Aitken*.

The back garden of the harbourside house at West Cowes of Sir Max Aitken was the setting for the naming ceremony, with the lifeboat moored off the private jetty and dressed overall. Major General Sir Robert Pigot, Bt, a member of the Committee of Management of the RNLI and president of the Isle of Wight Lifeboat Board, said it was fitting that the ceremony should take place at Cowes where Sir Max had sailed for many years with great success.

The Right Honourable Lord Robens, a trustee of the Beaverbrook Foundation, handed the lifeboat over to the RNLI, and the boat was accepted by the Duke of Atholl, chairman of the RNLI. A short service of dedication followed, conducted by the Rev Canon John Beam, Vicar of St Mary, Cowes, assisted by the Rev Brian Day, and the Rev Canon James Walsh. After the blessing, Lady Aitken pressed the button to break the champagne bottle and christen the lifeboat.

Sir Max Aitken served for more than twenty years in the Relief Fleet, gaining a fine record and saving more than 100 lives at stations throughout the UK and Ireland. Her first relief duty after the naming ceremony was at Torbay and she spent much of the early 1980s in the south-west, relieving at Falmouth, St Mary's, Weymouth and then Newhaven before going north in July 1986 to the west coast of Scotland.

Between July 1986 and March 1987 *Sir Max Aitken* was on relief duty at Mallaig, and she was involved in a very fine rescue. On 21 August 1986 she launched to the fishing vessel *LBP*. The Y boat was launched from which two lifeboat crew boarded the casualty, but when the casualty slid off the rocks and sank, the two lifeboatmen and three fishermen were left in the water. Lifeboatman Ian MacNaughton saved one of the fisherman and all five men were recovered onto the lifeboat. Following this service, the Thanks on Vellum was accorded to Ian MacNaughton.

On 30 September 1988, while on relief at Campbeltown, *Sir Max Aitken* was used to save the three crew from the fishing vessel *John Hannah VC*, a service for which the Thanks on Vellum was accorded to Coxswain/Mechanic Alexander Gilchrist.

In November 2002 *Sir Max Aitken* was taken out of the Relief Fleet and placed on the sale list. In February 2003 she was sold to Tenby Marine Services, in Pembrokeshire, was renamed *Maximus* and used as a safety boat at Pendine firing range. In 2006 she was sold again and by 2007 had moved to Essex, where she was kept near South Woodham Ferrers, moored off north bank of river Crouch near to Brandy Hole Yacht Club between Hullbridge and Fambridge, and employed for bird watching trips.

▲ Underway during a relief duty off Scotland.
(By courtesy of the RNLI)

▼ Torbay: on relief moored in Brixham harbour,
August 1984. (Nicholas Leach)

Robert Edgar

OFFICIAL NUMBER
1073

YEAR BUILT
1981

BUILDER
Halmatic Ltd hull, fit out
by William Osborne Ltd,
Littlehampton

YARD NO
WO 2305

WEIGHT
32 tons 12 cwt

COST
£328,860

DONOR
Gifts from Mrs Esme S. Edgar
and Mr Anthony Edgar

STATIONS
St Mary's (Scilly)
27 Jun 1981 – Dec 1997
(121/84)
Relief Fleet
5 Dec 1997 – 26 Aug 1999
(14/0)
Weymouth
4 Sep 1999 – 16 Jul 2002
(70/1)

DISPOSAL
Sold out of service in Feb 2003
to Brian A. Angliss, Rue de la
Folie, Toreval, Guernsey, via
Babcock Disposal Services

As the Arun build programme gathered momentum in the early 1980s, a decision was made to allocate one to the Isles of Scilly station at St Mary's, twenty-eight miles off the south-west tip of Cornwall, where the lifeboat had hitherto been slipway launched. A mooring in the middle of the harbour was found, and the boathouse was converted to take a wooden boarding boat.

The Arun for St Mary's, *Robert Edgar*, was fitted out by William Osborne in 1980 and completed in June 1981 ready for crew training and trials out of the RNLI Depot at Poole. She left Poole on 20 June and her passage west to the Scillies took two days. After a further five days of crew training for the St Mary's crew, she was placed on station.

The new lifeboat, donated by Mrs Esme Edgar and her son, Anthony Edgar, had been formally named by Mrs Edgar in memory of her late husband at a quiet ceremony at Poole on 15 June 1981. The handing over ceremony and dedication service were held on St Mary's Quay on 15 September 1981 in the presence of HRH The Duchess of Kent. The president of the station, W. C. T. Mumford, opened proceedings by welcoming guests to the ceremony, and the lifeboat was handed over to the RNLI by Mr Edgar. She was accepted by Captain T. A. Buckley and a service of dedication followed.

Robert Edgar served at St Mary's for more than sixteen years and performed several noteworthy rescues. On 22 June 1982 she was used to save two people from the yacht *Concerto*, which had a broken rudder in a south-westerly storm, high seas and heavy rain squalls, with the Thanks on Vellum being accorded to Coxswain Matthew Lethbridge for this rescue.

Robert Edgar was involved in a bronze medal-winning service on 12 September 1993 after the yacht *Bacarole* was swamped by heavy seas in very shallow waters of Porth Cressa Bay in severe gale force nine winds. The sole occupant was saved in difficult conditions which made towing the vessel impossible. He was hauled on board the lifeboat just as his yacht was engulfed by breaking surf and sank. The bronze medal was awarded to Coxswain Barry Bennett.

In December 1997 *Robert Edgar* was replaced at St Mary's by a new 17m Severn class lifeboat, and she left the station on 2 December 1997 for Pendennis Shipyard at Falmouth. She was reallocated to the Relief Fleet, in which she served for almost two years operating at, amongst other places, Dover (1997), Hartlepool (1998) and Humber (1998). In September 1999 she was sent to Weymouth to become station lifeboat, replacing the older Arun 54-04 *Tony Vandervell*. She spent almost three years there and gained a creditable record of service before being replaced by another new 17m Severn lifeboat in July 2002.

She left Weymouth in July 2002 and was placed on the sale list. She was sold out of service in 2003 to Brian A. Angliss, of Guernsey who had her shipped to New Zealand for use as a diving boat. In April 2003 she called at Ramsgate on her way to Tilbury, from where she was shipped to New Zealand via a container ship. In New Zealand she was kept at Tutukaka Marina, about 100 miles north of Auckland. Although in private hands, she is at the disposal of the New Zealand Coast Guard should she be needed for any offshore rescue work, mainly at the top dive site in the area, The Poor Knights Islands, fourteen miles offshore.

▲ On trials before entering service, 1981.
(By courtesy of the RNLI)

▼ Weymouth: putting out on exercise,
May 2001. (Nicholas Leach)

52-19

Marie Winstone

OFFICIAL NUMBER
1076

YEAR BUILT
1981

BUILDER
Halmatic Ltd hull, fit out by W. A. Souter, Cowes

YARD NO
—

WEIGHT
32 tons

COST
£344,097

DONOR
Gift from Mrs Marie Winstone, Sheffield

STATIONS
Fishguard
25 Aug 1981 – Sep 1994 (138/33)
Torbay
3 Feb 1995 – Oct 2001 (280/63)
Relief Fleet
30 Oct 2001 – Dec 2002 (3/0)

DISPOSAL
Sold out of service on 1 Oct 2002 to the Finland Lifeboat Service

The nineteenth Arun to be built was the second to be funded by Mrs Marie Winstone, of Sheffield, who had, the previous year, provided the boat for Holyhead, *Hyman Winstone*. This second Arun was named after the donor herself and allocated to another Welsh station, Fishguard, where she became the station's first lifeboat to be kept afloat. A special mooring pen was provided by the British Railways Board during harbour improvements, and this proved an ideal berth for the Arun.

The boat was fitted out by Souter Shipyard at Cowes, on the Isle of Wight, and arrived at Fishguard in August 1981 after a passage from the RNLI Depot at Poole. She was christened at Fishguard harbour by HRH The Duke of Kent at a ceremony held on 27 October 1981. Dr P. J. Croxford, chairman of Fishguard station, opened the ceremony, welcomed the Duke and mentioned how delighted Fishguard was to meet 'the legendary lady', Mrs Winstone, and pointed out that in the bay was not only the lifeboat to be named that day but also *Hyman Winstone*, which was in attendance from Holyhead.

The RNLI Chairman, the Duke of Atholl, received the lifeboat, and formally handed her into the care of the Fishguard branch via the station's honorary secretary, D. R. Williams. The service of dedication was conducted by the Very Rev Lawrence Bowen, assisted by the Rev Canon Lynn Griffiths, the Rev Father J. Jackson and the Rev Emlyn Jones. After praising Mrs Winstone's generosity, the Duke named the lifeboat.

Marie Winstone served at Fishguard for just over thirteen years and undertook many services during that time. In September 1994 she was replaced by one of the first 14m Trent lifeboats to go on station and was then reallocated to Torbay in place of the third of the Aruns, which had served Torbay since 1975. She left Fishguard on 24 September 1994 and was taken to Falmouth Boat Co to be refurbished prior to going to her new station. She left the Falmouth yard on 3 February 1995 and reached Brixham the same day to be immediately placed in service as Torbay lifeboat.

During her time at Torbay, where she served for six years, *Marie Winstone* gained a fine record of service. She was involved in a fine service on 1 January 1998 after the tanker *Santa Anna* ran aground just over three miles north of Brixham. The lifeboat, in heavy seas and a southerly gale, assisted the vessel, with the lifeboat crew making efforts to attach tow lines from the casualty to, firstly, the fishing boat *Marbella*, and later the Coastguard tug *Far Minerva*, which arrived on scene just after 9pm.

Once the tow had been secured, the tug pulled the tanker clear of the rocks while the lifeboat stood by. By 1am on 2 January *Santa Anna* had been safely anchored in Torbay, and the lifeboat was released to return to station. For his initiative and excellent seamanship throughout this rescue, Coxswain David Hurford was sent a framed letter of appreciation from the Chairman of the RNLI.

After more than six years at Torbay, *Marie Winstone* was replaced by a new 17m Severn class lifeboat and was transferred to the Relief Fleet, in which she served for a further year before being earmarked for disposal. She was sold out of service on 1 October 2002 to the Finnish Lifeboat Service, Suomen Meripelastusseura, and entered service in Finland in early 2003. She was stationed in Kaskinen, a small village in west Finland between Vaasa and Pori, and, in a new livery, was renamed *PR Torbay*.

▲ Fishguard: leaving the pen to meet her successor,
the 14m Trent Blue Peter VII. (Nicholas Leach)

▼ Torbay: on exercise off Brixham harbour while
stationed at Torbay, June 1996. (Nicholas Leach)

52-20

Duchess of Kent

OFFICIAL NUMBER
1077

YEAR BUILT
1981

BUILDER
Halmatic Ltd hull, fit out
by William Osborne Ltd,
Littlehampton

YARD NO
WO 2400

WEIGHT
31 tons 16 cwt

COST
£357,298

DONOR
United Grand Lodge of The
Freemasons of England

STATIONS
Relief Fleet
27 Apr 1982 – Oct 2002
(215/71)

DISPOSAL
Sold out of service on 30 Apr
2003 to SANAS, Madeira

In 1980 another Arun, the twentieth, was allocated to the Relief Fleet. The lifeboat was fitted out by William Osborne at Littlehampton during 1980 and 1981, and in September 1981 began her trials programme, including her self-righting trial. Her initial trials were completed in November 1981, and her final trails lasted from 6 to 16 January 1982, which ended with her acceptance trials.

After the trials, she was taken to the RNLI Depot at Poole, where further trials were undertaken in January 1982, and in February she went on her first relief duty. This took her to Tynemouth, where she served from 5 February until 27 March, when she was taken to Robson's Boatyard at South Shields and stored until 22 April. She was then taken to London for her naming ceremony and to attend the RNLI's Annual General Meeting.

Funded by the United Grand Lodge of The Freemasons of England and named *Duchess of Kent*, she was the third Arun to be built for the Relief Fleet. The naming ceremony was held on 27 April 1982, at the Jubilee Gardens, South Bank, London, and was attended by both the Duke and Duchess of Kent, as well as many RNLI branch and guild members. In his welcoming speech, the Duke of Atholl, chairman of the RNLI, said: 'It is unusual for a lifeboat naming ceremony to take place in our capital city but in this Maritime England Year, most appropriate, for we are here today on the banks of the Thames – a river which has flowed through our maritime history.'

The Duke of Kent then handed over the lifeboat, which was the latest of ten funded by the Masons. The Rt Rev George Reindorp, Honorary Assistant Bishop of London, led the service of dedication, assisted by Rev Principal Martin Cressey and Father Gerald

Burke, after which the Duke of Atholl called upon the Duchess of Kent to name the lifeboat, and the Duchess expressed her appreciation of having a lifeboat bear her name.

After her naming, *Duchess of Kent* began her relief duties in earnest, going to Port St Mary on May 1982, and staying there until 10 October 1982. She next went to Campbeltown, and then across to Portrush. Further service saw her at Campbeltown (1984) again, Mallaig (January to May 1984), Port St Mary (September 1984 to May 1985) and Barra Island (May to December 1985). In 1986 and 1987 she was on the south coast of England, at St Mary's and Penlee, before undertaking duties at Fishguard and Barry Dock.

Relief duties during the late 1990s took *Duchess of Kent* to Scotland, and she had stints at Troon, Barra Island, Stornoway, Islay and Campbeltown (all in 1990). She later went to Donaghadee, Ballycotton, Howth, Rosslare Harbour and Portrush, before returning to Scotland for duties at Islay (1997), the newly-opened station at Tobermory (1997), Troon (1998), and Barra Island (1998). In 1999 she went to Stornoway, Thurso and Lochinver, and in 2000 she undertook short stints at Dunbar, Lochinver and Stromness.

In October 2002 *Duchess of Kent* was withdrawn from service after twenty years in the Relief Fleet. She was sold out of service in April 2003 to SANAS, Madeira, for £130,000, and was shipped to her new home on board a P&O Nedlloyd container ship in November 2003. In Madeira she was stored out of the water at Canical for several years awaiting engine repairs and government permission to set up a rescue service. By 2009 she had been renamed *Salvador-Do-Mar* and, registered in Funchal, entered service operating from Funchal or Santa Cruz.

▲ Campbeltown: on relief duty,
April 1983. (Nicholas Leach)

▼ Dunbar: on relief duty, attending Anstruther Lifeboat
Day, July 2000. (Nicholas Leach)

Davina and Charles Matthews Hunter

OFFICIAL NUMBER
1078

YEAR BUILT
1982

BUILDER
Halmatic Ltd hull, fit out
by William Osborne Ltd,
Littlehampton

YARD NO
WO 2450

WEIGHT
31 tons 1 cwt

COST
£353,209

DONOR
Legacy of Miss Lilian Ferguson
Hunter, in memory of her
parents

STATIONS
Mallaig
16 Jul 1982 – Jan 2001
(309/44)
Relief Fleet
Jan 2001 – Jun 2003 (36/2)

DISPOSAL
Sold out of service on 15 Jul
2003 to ICE-SAR Iceland

The RNLI continued ordering Aruns in the early 1980s and the twenty-first boat was allocated to the Mallaig station on Scotland's west coast. She was fitted out during 1981 at William Osborne's yard and, following crew training and passage from the RNLI Depot at Poole, arrived at her station on 9 July 1982.

Before her naming ceremony she was called out on service several times. One call involved Coxswain David McMinn and his crew on service in the new lifeboat for more than twenty-four hours and another earned a formal letter of appreciation from the Chief Constable of the Northern Constabulary.

Funded from the legacy of Miss Lilian Ferguson Hunter, the new lifeboat was named *Davina and Charles Matthews Hunter* in memory of the donor's parents at a ceremony at Mallaig on 11 September 1982. The event was attended by many local people, guests and civic dignitaries. The lifeboat was named by Charles M. Hunter, who was acting as the donors' representative. In accepting the Arun on behalf of the RNLI, Sir Charles McGrigor, a vice-president and convener of the Scottish Lifeboat Council, delivered her into the care of Mallaig station branch; in turn, she was accepted by the honorary secretary Archie MacLellan.

Rev A. McGowan, minister of the parish of Mallaig and the Small Isles, supported by Canon E. MacInnes of St Cumin's Church, Morar, conducted the service and dedication. Then Mr Hunter named the boat, and the Arun slipped her moorings and headed out into the harbour where she was escorted by an air sea rescue helicopter from RAF Leuchars.

Davina and Charles Matthews Hunter gained a fine record of service at Mallaig and was involved in many rescues. Her most noteworthy service took place on 27 October 1988 after the fishing boat *Galilean* got into difficulties on the southern shore of Loch Nevis. The lifeboat put out at 6.32pm in rapidly deteriorating weather and headed into northerly storm force winds and heavy seas at slow speed. At one point, Assistant Mechanic George Laurie was washed overboard by a large wave but fortunately, along with the rest of the crew, he was secured by his lifeline and so he was quickly pulled back on board by his colleagues.

Eight minutes after launching the lifeboat found the casualty dragging two anchors. In atrocious conditions, with force eleven northerly winds and visibility seriously reduced by driving spray, the coxswain was concerned about submerged rocks and so the lifeboat was manoeuvred carefully towards the anchored casualty. The crew passed the towline across by hand and, once it was secure, the lifeboat went astern, taking up the strain, and pulling the vessel clear.

The lifeboat arrived off Mallaig Harbour to find the conditions so bad that entering the harbour with a tow was too dangerous, so the coxswain towed the casualty to Inverie in Loch Nevis where, at 9.49pm, the casualty was secured. For this difficult rescue, Coxswain/Mechanic Thomas Ralston was awarded the bronze medal.

In January 2001 *Davina and Charles Matthews Hunter* was replaced at Mallaig by a new Severn lifeboat, and she then served for almost two and a half years as a Relief lifeboat. In June 2003 she was taken out of service and the following month sold to ICE-SAR, the Icelandic lifeboat service. She was renamed *Einar Sigurjónsson* and placed on station at Hafnarfjörður, near Reykjavik, in August 2003.

▲ On trials shortly after being built.
(By courtesy of the RNLI)

▼ Mallaig: moored in the harbour,
August 1997. (Nicholas Leach)

Ralph and Bonella Farrant

OFFICIAL NUMBER
1081

YEAR BUILT
1982

BUILDER
Halmatic Ltd hull, fit out by W. A. Souter, Cowes

YARD NO
—

WEIGHT
30 tons 14 cwt

COST
£350,869

DONOR
RNLI General Funds, named in honour of Major General Ralph H. Farrant, CB

STATIONS
Relief Fleet
26 Jul 1982 – 1994 (226/106)
Fenit
18 Aug 1994 – Feb 1999 (91/49)
Relief Fleet
1999 – Aug 2003 (116/24)

DISPOSAL
Sold out of service in Nov 2005 to China Rescue & Salvage Bureau

*R*alph and Bonella Farrant was the fourth Arun to be built for the Relief Fleet. Her hull was ordered in June 1981 from Halmatic, and at the end of December it was moved to Souter's Yard at Cowes for fitting out. Construction work was completed by March 1982 and machinery trials were conducted during April and May 1982. Acceptance trials took place on 16 June 1982 and the boat was then taken to the RNLI Depot in Poole. After further trials, *Ralph and Bonella Farrant* was officially placed in the Relief Fleet on 26 July 1982.

The first Relief duty for the new lifeboat was a short stint, lasting just three days, at Torbay, followed by a couple of months at Yarmouth, Isle of Wight. On 24 September 1982 she returned to Souter's to be prepared for her naming ceremony. After the naming she went back to Yarmouth for a six-month spell until 11 March 1983.

Her naming took place at the RNLI Depot at Poole on 8 October 1982 with Rear Admiral W. J. Graham, director of the RNLI, opening the proceedings. The boat was named in honour of Major General Ralph H. Farrant, RNLI chairman from 1975 to 1979, and Mrs Farrant. Among the audience were many of General and Mrs Farrant's relations and friends, colleagues and RNLI staff.

In handing the new lifeboat over to the Institution the Duke of Atholl, chairman of the RNLI said, 'One of the most splendid of RNLI traditions is to name a lifeboat as a tribute to those who have served as chairmen of the Institution. During his time as chairman, General Farrant visited lifeboat stations throughout Britain and Ireland, and it is fitting that this lifeboat will serve in the Relief Fleet.'

Commander Bruce Cairns, chief of operations, accepted the lifeboat on behalf of the RNLI and the service of dedication was led by the Rev Peter G. Hardman, Rector of Wareham. After a few words from Major General Farrant, Mrs Farrant named the lifeboat *Ralph and Bonella Farrant*. General and Mrs Farrant were escorted to 'their' lifeboat by the chairman and the director, and they went afloat for a short trip.

She served at many stations during the 1980s, including St Peter Port, Humber, Penlee, St Mary's, Falmouth, Fishguard, Penlee, Weymouth, Torbay, Dover, Plymouth, Newhaven and Yarmouth. In the 1990s she went to Weymouth, St Peter Port, Penlee and Falmouth (1990); Humber and Tynemouth (1991); Dover and Humber (1992); Humber (1993); and Tynemouth (1993-94).

At this time, the RNLI was expanding rescue provision in Ireland, and in 1994 opened a new station at Fenit, covering Tralee Bay, in the south-west. *Ralph and Bonella Farrant* was allocated to the new station and during June 1994 she was taken from the RNLI Depot at Poole to her new station, via overnight stops at Salcombe, St Peter Port, St Mary's, Dunmore East and Baltimore. She arrived on Ireland's west coast on 29 June 1994, and after further training became operational in August 1994.

Ralph and Bonella Farrant spent almost five years at Fenit, until being replaced by a new lifeboat in February 1999 and once again being placed in the Relief Fleet. A further four years as a Relief lifeboat, including spells at Plymouth and Dover, brought her career total to over 400 services.

Sold out of service in November 2005 to the China Rescue & Salvage Bureau, she was shipped from the UK in April 2006, via a container ship from Felixstowe. Renamed *Huaying 393*, she was placed in service at Fuzhou.

▲ Fenit: on exercise, August 1995.
(Nicholas Leach)

▼ Participating in the RNLI's 175th anniversary
celebrations at Poole, June 1999. (Nicholas Leach)

Margaret Frances Love

OFFICIAL NUMBER
1082

YEAR BUILT
1981

BUILDER
Halmatic Ltd hull, fit out
by William Osborne Ltd,
Littlehampton

YARD NO
WO 2510

WEIGHT
30 tons 12 cwt

COST
£362,214

DONOR
Bequests of Mr Frank Love,
Ewhurst, Surrey, in memory of
his wife Ada Marian, and Lady
Frances Murphy, in memory of
her daughter Margaret Frances
Murphy, Dun Laoghaire, with
other gifts and legacies

STATIONS
Valentia
14 Mar 1983 – Nov 1996
(192/73)
Barry Dock
11 May 1997 – 2 Aug 2003
(129/10)

DISPOSAL
Sold out of service in Jul 2005
to China Rescue & Salvage
Bureau

The key lifeboat station of Valentia, on Ireland's south-west corner, was allocated the Arun lifeboat *Margaret Frances Love* in 1981. The lifeboat was fitted out by William Osborne at Littlehampton during 1981 with trials in early 1982. In February 1982 crew training was undertaken and during March the lifeboat was sailed to Valentia.

The new lifeboat was provided by the generous bequests of Frank Love, in memory of his wife Ada Marian and their daughter Margaret Frances, and Lady Frances Murphy of Dun Laoghaire. Named *Margaret Frances Love*, she was placed on station at Valentia on 14 March 1983.

The naming ceremony took place on a windy and rainy 17 September 1983 at Knightstown, Valentia. The proceedings were opened by Father Denis Costello, the branch chairman, who extended a warm welcome to Lt Cdr Brian Miles, a past divisional inspector of lifeboats in Ireland and then deputy director of the Institution.

The Arun was handed into the care of the station by Clayton Love, a vice-president of the RNLI, and P. J. Gallagher, the honorary secretary, accepted the first Arun lifeboat to be stationed in the Republic of Ireland. The Most Rev Dr Kevin McNamara, Bishop of Kerry, and the Rev Brian Lougheed, blessed and dedicated the lifeboat. Then Lady Killanin named the boat *Margaret Frances Love* which, with the breaking of the bottle of champagne, slipped her moorings for a short demonstration.

Margaret Frances Love undertook almost 200 services while at Valentia and completed a very fine rescue on the afternoon of 12 January 1985 after the fishing vessel *Fortune Hunter*, with three people aboard, was reported overdue. The weather was fair when *Margaret Frances Love* set out at 7.50pm. *Fortune Hunter*, which had no radio on board, had left Cromane at 1.30am and Coxswain Murphy therefore decided to search first in the Ventry area. The lifeboat crew found the fishing boat, disabled, and in shallow water close to a cliff face.

The wind was gusting to force six, but a tow line was passed across and the fishing boat was towed clear and then taken to Dingle. A letter, signed by Cdr Bruce Cairns, chief of operations, was sent to the Valentia station thanking Coxswain Sean Murphy and his crew for their efforts.

After just over thirteen years on service at Valentia, *Margaret Frances Love* was replaced by a new 17m Severn class lifeboat, and the Arun was reallocated to Barry Dock. She left Valentia in January 1997 and travelled to North Wales. After some minor repairs at Dickie's Boatyard, Bangor, she set off for Barry Dock on 29 April 1997, stopping overnight at Wicklow and Fishguard, and arriving at Barry on 1 May 1997. She undertook crew training passages to Kilmore Quay, Howth and Fishguard, as well as a public relations visit to Bristol from 2 to 4 May 1997, before she returned to Barry on 10 May and was placed on station the following day.

Margaret Frances Love served at Barry Dock for six years, launching on service over 100 times. She was replaced in August 2003 by another Arun, and was taken to the RNLI Depot at Poole. She remained at Poole until a sale to the China Rescue & Salvage Bureau was completed in July 2005. She was then transported to China on board a COSCO container ship, leaving Felixstowe on 5 August 2005. In China, she was renamed *Huaying 398* and stationed at Yangkou, Nantong City, Jiangsu.

▲ Valentia: on moorings off the village of
Knightstown, 26 June 1991. (Tony Denton)

▼ Barry Dock: leaving harbour on exercise on a misty
Sunday morning, November 1997. (Nicholas Leach)

52-24

Mabel Alice

OFFICIAL NUMBER
1085

YEAR BUILT
1983

BUILDER
Halmatic Ltd hull, fit out by
Fairey Marine, Cowes

YARD NO
FM 715

WEIGHT
30 tons 12 cwt

COST
£345,467

DONOR
Gift of Sir David Robinson in
honour of his wife, and as a
tribute to Penlee

STATIONS
Penlee
8 May 1983 – Feb 2003
(275/83)

DISPOSAL
Sold out of service in Mar 2004
to Strathclyde Joint Police
Board, Glasgow, Scotland

When the Penlee lifeboat *Solomon Browne* was tragically lost on service on 19 December 1981, in the aftermath of the tragedy the RNLI determined that the best long-term replacement would be an Arun lifeboat moored in Newlyn harbour, a couple of miles from the boathouse at Penlee Point where the station's previous lifeboats, including *Solomon Browne*, had been based.

So a new 52ft Arun was ordered for the station, and, between April and November 1982, it was fitted out at Fairey Marine's yard at Cowes. During spring 1983, the new boat was taken to the RNLI Depot at Poole, and following a week of crew training was sailed to Cornwall by hew new crew. She arrived at Newlyn in May 1983 having called at Mousehole, where most of the crew lived, during the final leg of the passage.

The new lifeboat was provided by Sir David Robinson, of Newmarket, and was named *Mabel Alice* in honour of his wife and as a tribute to the Penlee lifeboatmen who lost their lives in *Solomon Browne*. She was named at a ceremony held at Newlyn on 18 July 1983 by HRH The Duke of Kent, President of the Institution. The quayside was packed with people from all over the country to witness the event, with the coxswains from every Cornish station present.

Captain R. E. Goodman, president of Penlee station branch, opened the proceedings, and Colin Evans delivered a personal message from David Robinson, the donor, in which he sent his regrets that neither he nor his wife could be present. The Duke of Atholl, chairman of the RNLI, thanked Mr Evans for presenting the lifeboat and D. L. Johnson, honorary secretary, accepted the boat on behalf of the station. The service of dedication was led by the Right Rev Bishop Michael, Bishop of St Germans. The Duke of Kent then christened *Mabel Alice*, with the champagne bottle breaking over her bows, while a helicopter from RNAS Culdrose flew overhead.

Mabel Alice served at Penlee for almost twenty years, and undertook her most challenging service on 6 December 1994 when she went to the fishing vessel *Julian Paul*, which was disabled with a fouled propeller four miles south-west of the Longships light in force nine winds and appalling sea conditions. Sennen Cove's Mersey class lifeboat *The Four Boys* was the first to be called out to help the casualty, but the weather was so bad *Mabel Alice* was also tasked to assist. A tow was rigged, and at one stage both lifeboats were needed to make progress.

The service lasted almost ten hours, mostly in complete darkness, and with winds gusting to 82mph. Both crews suffered from seasickness, but both coxswains showed skill in establishing the tows and cooperated fully with each other to bring the vessel safely into Newlyn. Following the service Coxswain/Mechanic Neil Brockman of Penlee and Coxswain/Mechanic Terry George of Sennen Cove were each awarded the bronze medal.

Mabel Alice served at Penlee for twenty years until being replaced in February 2003. She was then sold in March 2004 to Strathclyde Joint Police Board for use as a police boat. After a survey at Souter's Shipyard at Cowes, she was taken to Glasgow renamed *Strathclyde* and based at Great Harbour, Greenock, with her superstructure painted yellow. In late 2008 the Police Board sold her to Andy Iannetta, who took her to Portishead Marina for use as a pleasure boat, reinstating her original name and maintaining her lifeboat appearance.

▲ On trials before entering service, 1983.
(By courtesy of the RNLI)

▼ Penlee: moored in Newlyn harbour,
August 1992. (Nicholas Leach)

A. J. R. and L. G. Uridge

OFFICIAL NUMBER
1086

YEAR BUILT
1983

BUILDER
Halmatic Ltd hull, fit out by William Osborne Ltd, Littlehampton

YARD NO
WO 2590

WEIGHT
30 tons 15 cwt

COST
£369,078

DONOR
Bequest of Lionel George Uridge and a gift from the late Mrs Alice Audrey Burnley

STATIONS
Relief Fleet
15 Sep 1983 – 15 Mar 2003 (345/111)
Torbay (temporary duty)
17 Apr 1994 – Feb 1995 (43/26)

DISPOSAL
Sold out of service in Aug 2003 to Finland Lifeboat Service

The twenty-fifth Arun to be built was another allocated to the Relief Fleet, and she served her whole career as a Relief lifeboat. She was ordered in early 1982 and in September 1982 her hull was taken to William Osborne's yard to be fitted out. Work on her was finished in mid-May 1983, after which she spent two months on trials out of Littlehampton. Her initial trials were completed on 22 July 1983, and after she had passed her forty-hour trials five days later she was taken into service and immediately sent to Portrush, in Northern Ireland, for a first Relief duty. She arrived at Portrush on 1 August and stayed for a month, departing on 1 September and heading for Newhaven.

She arrived at Newhaven on 6 September 1983 ready for her naming ceremony the following day. Newhaven had been chosen for the ceremony because it was the nearest lifeboat station to the Lewes home of Miss C. G. Uridge, who was to name the new boat *A. J. R. and L. G. Uridge* in memory of her father and brother. The boat had been funded from the legacy of Mr L. G. Uridge and gift of Mrs A. A. Burnley. The Uridge family had been associated with the lifeboat service for many years. Mr A. J. R. Uridge founded the RNLI's Lewes Branch in 1924 and was awarded the gold badge in 1931. His son, also Miss Uridge's brother, Lionel, carried on the family tradition in Lewes, serving as branch honorary secretary and treasurer between 1948 and 1964.

At the ceremony, Lieut Cdr Brian Miles, the RNLI's deputy director, opened the proceedings and the new lifeboat was formally presented to the RNLI by Mr W. W. Kenward, representing the trustees of the L. G. Uridge Estate. The service of dedication was conducted by the Rev

J. G. P. Habgood, after which Miss Uridge named the lifeboat.

After her naming, *A. J. R. and L. G. Uridge* officially entered the Relief fleet on 15 September 1983 and served for a couple of weeks at Newhaven before returning to William Osborne's yard for some minor repairs and maintenance work. On 19 October 1983 she went to Holyhead for another duty, and stayed there for eight months, during which time she launched seven times on service, and saved four lives.

She spent six months at Fishguard from June 1984 to January 1985, saving thirteen lives, and then was at Dover for much of 1985. There she was involved in an unusual service to the cross-Channel hovercraft *Princess Margaret,* which had collided with the harbour arm in bad weather on the afternoon of 30 March 1985. *A. J. R. and L. G. Uridge* was quickly on scene, saved five people from the water and landed a further eighty-three passengers from the hovercraft.

Her next Relief duties during the late 1980s took her to Scotland, and she served at Lerwick, Stromness, Aith and Thurso before going to Ireland and serving at Portrush and Donaghadee. During the 1990s she served at stations in the south-west, including Falmouth, Penlee, St Mary's, Plymouth, Weymouth and Torbay, and she also went to Ballyglass, Rosslare and Holyhead. In 1999 she spent six months at Plymouth, then went to Penlee, Barry Dock and Donaghadee.

As the RNLI began to replace and sell the Aruns, *A. J. R. and L. G. Uridge* was taken out of service in March 2003 and placed on the sale list, having been in service for twenty years during which time she had saved over 100 lives. She was sold in August 2003 to the Finland Lifeboat Service and, as *PR Hebe*, was stationed at Kemi.

▲ On trials before entering service, 1983.
(By courtesy of the RNLI)

▼ Torbay: on relief duty moored in Brixham harbour, October 1994. (Nicholas Leach)

52-26

St Brendan

The important station at Rosslare Harbour, on the south-east corner of Ireland, was allocated a new 52ft Arun lifeboat in 1983. The Rosslare boat was the twenty-sixth Arun to be built and she was fitted out by William Osborne, of Littlehampton, after her hull had been moulded at Halmatic Ltd.

Named *St Brendan*, she arrived at the port on Wednesday 4 April 1984 after a three-day passage from the RNLI's Depot at Poole in Dorset, via Falmouth, Newlyn and Fishguard. Coxswain Wilf Stafford, Second Coxswain Seamus McCormack, Mechanic Matt Wickham, and crew members Tony Kehoe and Brendan Pitt brought the new boat home after two weeks of training at Poole. Also on board during the passage were Tony Course, RNLI Divisional Inspector for Ireland, and Robbie Robinson, the area's District Engineer.

The new lifeboat was officially placed on station on 1 June 1984, having performed her first service on 25 May 1984, when she towed in the local motor fishing vessel *Duncairn*, which had got into difficulty after her propeller had been fouled by nets.

Funded from RNLI general funds, *St Brendan* was formally named at a ceremony on 28 June 1985 at Rosslare Harbour by Mrs Patricia Mitchell, wife of Jim Mitchell, Minister for Communications. Proceedings were opened by Cecil Miller, Chairman of the Branch, and the lifeboat was delivered into the care of the branch by Clayton Love Jnr, a vice-president of the RNLI. The service of dedication was conducted by the Rt Rev Noel Willoughby and the Most Rev Brendan Comiskey. Mrs Mitchell christened the lifeboat, which then slipped her moorings and took invited guests for a short trip to sea.

St Brendan was moored for most of her career in a series of boarding pens within Rosslare ferry port. When she arrived, a new pen had been built for her, and this was formally opened during her naming ceremony. In 1996 another new berth was provided and involved the dredging of the harbour, provision of a dolphin to moor the boat alongside and an access bridge.

However, being in the confines of the ferry port could be hazardous. In strong winds and bad weather the ferries could drift while berthing, and on 9 September 2001 disaster struck when the Stena Line ferry *Köningin Beatrix* lost power manoeuvring onto her berth and accidentally hit lifeboat and lifeboat pen, destroying both. The ship ploughed into the bank in front of the lifeboat, causing substantial damage to the boat. It was the third time the lifeboat had been hit by one of the ferries during her time on station.

Although considerably damaged, *St Brendan* remained afloat, and was able to reach Kilmore Quay under her own power, for inspection the next day. But she was found to be beyond repair and was immediately taken out of service. It was an unfortunate end to *St Brendan's* career at Rosslare. During just over seventeen years on station, she completed 147 services and saved twenty-eight lives.

From Kilmore Quay, *St Brendan* was taken to Holyhead Boatyard, where she was taken out of the water and subsequently sold as scrap in February 2003, having been stripped of her engines and internal equipment. Despite being written off, she was purchased by a Manchester-based man who repaired her and renamed her *Irish Mist*. She was used as a dive boat with berths for seventeen, operating out of Holyhead, and with her superstructure painted gray.

▲ On trials shortly after being built. (By courtesy of the RNLI)

▼ Rosslare Harbour: at moorings in the ferry port. (Nicholas Leach)

52-27

Charles Brown

OFFICIAL NUMBER
1093

YEAR BUILT
1983

BUILDER
Halmatic Ltd hull, fit out
by William Osborne Ltd,
Littlehampton

YARD NO
WO 2650

WEIGHT
31 tons 11 cwt

COST
£383,638

DONOR
Gift of Mr David Robinson

STATIONS
Buckie
5 Apr 1984 – May 2003
(270/172)
Relief Fleet
May 2003 – 4 Jul 2005 (13/0)

DISPOSAL
Sold out of service in Nov 2005
to China Rescue & Salvage
Bureau

The twenty-seventh Arun to be built was the second to be donated by Mr David Robinson, who had already funded the Penlee lifeboat *Mabel Alice* in 1983. Named *Charles Brown* after a close friend and business associate of Mr Robinson, the new lifeboat was allocated to the Buckie station on the Banffshire coast. The lifeboat was fitted out by William Osborne at Littlehampton and, once completed, was taken to the RNLI Depot in early 1984. After training for the Buckie crew at the end of March 1984 had been completed, the lifeboat was taken to her new home up the west coast of England, making her first stop at Newlyn harbour where she was moored alongside *Mabel Alice*.

The passage saw the boat head north with overnight stops at Holyhead on Anglesey, Port St Mary on the Isle of Man, and Oban, which was the last overnight stop before the final leg of her journey. From Oban she was taken through the Caledonian Canal and on to Buckie, to be escorted home by the 48ft 6in Solent *Royal British Legion Jubilee*. On 5 April 1984 she was placed on service.

Charles Brown completed four services by the time of her naming ceremony on 25 August 1984. At the naming, the Duke of Atholl, chairman of the RNLI, delivered the lifeboat into the care of the station branch secretary and the service of dedication at the ceremony was conducted by the Rev J. R. Osbeck, assisted by Rev A. Barr and Rev T. N. Johnston. At the end of the ceremony, the lifeboat was named by Mrs Constance Brown, widow of Charles Brown.

During her time at Buckie, *Charles Brown* achieved an excellent record of service and is credited with saving 172 lives. She was involved in a particularly noteworthy episode on 17 July 1987

when, in force seven south-easterly winds and rough seas, she launched to the aid of two different vessels caught out by the heavy weather. First, she launched to the auxiliary yacht *Samphire*, which was twenty miles north of Macduff. The yacht had three persons on board and the sails had been damaged, so the lifeboat escorted her to safety. Two hours later, *Charles Brown* was at again sea, this time going to the aid of the 50ft Swedish topsail schooner *Monsoon*, which had broken down five miles north-east of Portknockie. The casualty was found pitching heavily in the rough seas. A towline was rigged, but progress was slow in the heavy weather. Eventually the vessels neared the shore, and *Charles Brown* approached Burghead with the schooner in tow.

Once inside the harbour, the vessel was secured, and, as its four crew were found to be okay, *Charles Brown* returned to station. Following this service, in recognition of the teamwork and dedication displayed by Coxswain John Murray and his crew, a framed letter of thanks signed by the Duke of Atholl, chairman of the Institution, was presented to the station.

In 2003 *Charles Brown* was replaced at Buckie by a new 17m Severn lifeboat and she then spent a year in the Relief Fleet before being sold. During her time in Relief, she served briefly at Buckie along with other stations in Scotland, before being taken to the RNLI Depot at Poole for disposal.

She was sold out of service in November 2005 to the China Rescue & Salvage Bureau, becoming the latest lifeboat to be taken to China as deck cargo. She went on the container ship *Cosco Shanghai*, which sailed from Felixstowe. In China, she was renamed *Huaying 396* and become one of three former RNLI lifeboats based at Yan Tai

▲ On trials shortly after being built. (By courtesy of the RNLI)

▼ Buckie: on exercise off the harbour, August 1996. (Nicholas Leach)

Sir Max Aitken II

OFFICIAL NUMBER
1098

YEAR BUILT
1983

BUILDER
Halmatic Ltd hull, fit out by W. A.
Souter, Cowes

YARD NO
—

WEIGHT
31 tons

COST
£377,974

DONOR
The Beaverbrook Foundation

STATIONS
Stornoway
6 Mar 1984 – Feb 1999
(238/67)
Relief Fleet
3 Feb 1999 – 6 Aug 1999 (2/0)
Longhope
12 Aug 1999 – Jun 2004
(21/0)
Relief Fleet
Jun 2004 – 4 Jul 2005 (3/0)

DISPOSAL
Sold out of service in Nov 2005
to China Rescue & Salvage
Bureau

During the early 1980s the RNLI continued to build new Arun lifeboats for stations in Ireland and on Scotland's rugged west coast, and in 1982 an Arun was allocated to Stornoway, on Lewis in the Outer Hebrides. Named *Sir Max Aitken II,* the boat was fitted out at Cowes by W. A. Souter and completed in early December 1983, being taken to the RNLI Depot at Poole after passing her forty-hour trials.

Although allocated to Stornoway, the new lifeboat was officially named, on 23 February 1984, at Cowes on the Isle of Wight, rather than at her Lewis home. The boat was the second 52ft Arun to be funded by The Beaverbrook Foundation, of which Sir Max Aitken was chairman, and so for the second time in three years The Prospect, West Cowes, harbourside home of Sir Max, was the setting for a naming ceremony.

The boat was named by HRH Princess Alexandra, with Coxswain Malcolm MacDonald and other lifeboat crew from Stornoway on board her, and representatives from Stornoway's station branch and Ladies' Lifeboat Guild among the guests. Lord Robens, a trustee of the Beaverbrook Foundation, opened the proceedings, and the Duke of Atholl, chairman of the RNLI, handed the boat into the care of Stornoway station. Following the service of dedication led by the Rev Richard Parker, Princess Alexandra named the lifeboat.

Following her official naming, *Sir Max Aitken II* was taken to Lewis, where she was placed on station at Stornoway on 6 March 1984, and on 25 July 1984 she was formally rededicated at her station by the Rev Roderick Morrison. More than 500 friends and supporters of the station attended the event, with the chairman and former coxswain, Ian Maclean,

overseeing the proceedings.

One of the most dramatic rescues in which *Sir Max Aitken II* was involved took place on 13 February 1989, when she launched in hurricane force conditions to the assistance of the fishing vessel *Westward* and her crew of two. The vessel was dragging her anchor seawards off Holm Island and in considerable danger. In extremely difficult conditions, Coxswain Malcolm MacDonald manoeuvred the lifeboat close to the fishing boat and rescued the two crew. For his high standard of seamanship, leadership and courage Coxswain MacDonald was awarded the bronze medal, with Medal Service Certificates for the rest of the crew.

Although reallocated to Barry Dock in 1995, *Sir Max Aitken II* remained at Stornoway because of problems with the station's replacement Severn class lifeboat, one of the first boats of the new class. She did not leave Stornoway until February 1999, when a new 17m Severn was operational, after which she was placed in the Relief Fleet. She served as a Relief lifeboat for only six months, undertaking short duties at Tobermory, Montrose and Lochinver, before being reallocated to the Longhope station on Hoy in Orkney.

Between 6 and 12 August 1999 the Longhope crew undertook training on the new boat, which replaced a Tyne class lifeboat that had been slipway launched, and on 12 August she was placed on station. She served at Longhope for almost five years before being replaced by another Arun, 52-43 *The Queen Mother*, and was then again placed in the Relief Fleet.

After a year as a Relief lifeboat, she was placed on the sale list and in November 2005 was sold out of service to the China Rescue & Salvage Bureau. In China she was renamed *Huaying 397,* and was based at Guang Zhou.

▲ Stornoway: on exercise off the Isle of Lewis.
(By courtesy of Stornoway RNLI)

▼ Longhope: passing Cantick Head lighthouse while on exercise off Hoy, June 2004. (Nicholas Leach)

Joseph Rothwell Sykes and Hilda M.

OFFICIAL NUMBER
1099

YEAR BUILT
1983

BUILDER
Halmatic Ltd hull, fit out
by William Osborne Ltd,
Littlehampton

YARD NO
WO 2700

WEIGHT
31 tons

COST
£373,034

DONOR
Bequests of Mr J. Sykes, Mrs
Nora Sykes, Miss Doris Rothwell
and Miss Hilda M. Vyvyan

STATIONS
Stromness
15 Oct 1984 – 22 Oct 1998
(89/8)
Broughty Ferry
20 Jan 1999 – Apr 2001
(52/0)
Relief Fleet
7 Apr 2001 – 31 Dec 2002
(2/0)

DISPOSAL
Sold out of service in 2002 to
the Finland Lifeboat Service

As the Arun building programme gathered pace during the early 1980s, one was allocated to the Stromness station on Orkney Mainland in 1983 after it had been determined that a suitable mooring could be provided in the town's harbour. Hitherto the station's lifeboats had been slipway launched from a boathouse on the waterfront.

Fitted out by William Osborne at Littlehampton at a cost of approximately £370,000, *Joseph Rothwell Sykes and Hilda M.*, the boat allocated to Stromness, arrived in Orkney on 12 October 1984 after a passage from the RNLI Depot at Poole. She travelled north following a week of training at the RNLI's Depot at Poole for Coxswain W. Sinclair, Mechanic S. Taylor, Second Mechanic J. Adams and crew M. Flett and C. McIver. Lieut John Unwin, Divisional Inspector for North of Scotland, was in command for the passage.

The naming ceremony took place at Stromness on the afternoon of 22 August 1985. At the start of the ceremony, Mrs Stout, Chairman of the Community Council, presented a Township Plaque to the crew of

the lifeboat. The plaque, bearing the Coat of Arms of Stromness, was subsequently fixed to the lifeboat's superstructure. The service of dedication was conducted by the Rev R. S. Whiteford, after which Mrs Mary Milne, sister of the executor of the Sykes estate, formally named the lifeboat.

With official guests aboard and to the sound of three local pipers, the new lifeboat then went for a short trip to sea. The somewhat unusual name was a combination of two bequests, one from Miss Doris Rothwell, her sister Mrs Nora Sykes and her husband Joseph Sykes, which was to be used to provide the new lifeboat named *Joseph Rothwell Sykes*; and another from Mrs Hilda May Vyvyan, which was to be used for a lifeboat for Orkney named *Hilda* or *Hilda M.* These were combined to form the boat's name.

Joseph Rothwell Sykes and Hilda M served at Stromness for fourteen years, during which time she is credited with saving eight lives. She was replaced in October 1998 by a new 17m Severn class lifeboat. She was then used as a Relief lifeboat, spending a few days at Lochinver in late October 1998, before being reallocated to Broughty Ferry to replace one of the older Aruns. On 1 November 1998 she went to Buckie Boatyard to be overhauled, and was ready for her next duty in January 1999. She arrived at Broughty Ferry on 17 January and three days later was placed on station.

After just over two years there, she was replaced at Broughty by a new 14m Trent lifeboat and she then entered the Relief Fleet for the best part of two years before being placed on the sale list. She was sold in 2002 to the Finnish Lifeboat Service and, renamed *PR Janne Malen*, stationed at Uusikaupunki in western Finland.

▼ Naming ceremony at Stornoway, 22 August 1985.

▲ Stromness: leaving harbour on exercise,
August 1997. (Nicholas Leach)

▼ Broughty Ferry: at moorings in the river Tay,
August 1999. (Nicholas Leach)

52-030

Snolda

OFFICIAL NUMBER
1100

YEAR BUILT
1984

BUILDER
Fairey Marine, Cowes

YARD NO
FM 722

WEIGHT
32 tons 5 cwt

COST
£391,021

DONOR
Donations from various oil companies, together with local appeals and gifts

STATIONS
Aith
19 Jul 1986 – May 1998
(79/29)
Training Lifeboat
May 1998 – 16 Oct 2007 (0/0)

DISPOSAL
Sold out of service in Oct 2007 to ICE-SAR, Iceland

The Aruns built with glass reinforced plastic hulls had performed very well in service, and the material, innovative when introduced in the 1970s, was deemed a success. It had been proven over many years, but in the early 1980s an Arun was built from steel as a trial. At the time, the newly-designed 47ft Tyne class lifeboats were also being built from steel and so the RNLI already had steel lifeboats under construction.

FBM Marine Ltd agreed to go ahead with the steel-hulled Arun, and began work in May 1983. The boat took more than two years to build, and by the time it was completed in November 1985 it had been allocated to Aith in Shetland, the RNLI's most northerly station. Because this was a unique boat, she underwent many more trials than usual to determine the effect the different hull material had on her performance, with trials lasting from November 1985 to July 1986.

Named *Snolda*, she turned out to be the only steel-hulled Arun built by the RNLI, and her operational number – 52-030 – reflected this with the zero after the hyphen indicating a steel hull. To accommodate the new lifeboat at Aith, a special pier was constructed, which improved boarding facilities for the crew. *Snolda* served throughout her operational life at Aith, and had one of the largest sea areas to cover of any British lifeboat.

Training for the Aith crew was undertaken at Poole in July 1986, after which the new lifeboat was taken to Shetland on a training passage between 7 and 11 July. Following further crew training at Aith, *Snolda* was declared operational on 19 July 1986.

The new boat, which had been funded from donations by various oil companies together with the proceeds of a local appeal at Aith, was named on 25 July 1987 when, with a population of just 220, Aith played host to their Royal Highnesses the Prince and Princess of Wales and welcomed more than 600 guests for the ceremony and the opening of the pier. Alongside the new lifeboat lay the boat she was replacing, the 52ft Barnett *John and Frances Macfarlane,* and among other vessels paying tribute was the Norwegian lifeboat *Skomvaer III.*

The proceedings were opened by the Aith branch chairman, Dr Margaret Shimmin. Mr P. Everett, managing director of Shell UK, represented the donors and handed the lifeboat over to the Duke of Atholl, chairman of the RNLI, who in turn delivered her into the safe keeping of station honorary secretary, Mr D. Garrick. After the service of dedication, the Princess of Wales named the lifeboat *Snolda.*

In 1996 *Snolda* and her crew were involved in two fine services. On 7 February she rescued the crew of eleven and saved the 310-tonne Norwegian fishing vessel *Vindhammer* after a nine-hour tow to Sullom Voe in a severe gale and heavy seas, for which the Thanks Inscribed on Vellum was accorded to Coxswain Hylton Henry. And on 24 October the fishing vessel *Radiant Star II*, with a crew of five, was towed to safety, for which a framed letter of thanks was awarded to Coxswain Hylton Henry in recognition of his leadership and seamanship.

After being replaced at Aith in May 1998, she was used as a Relief lifeboat for a short period, with stints at Aberdeen in February 1999 and Dover in March 1999, before being reallocated to the training fleet. She was used as a training lifeboat until 2007 and was then sold out of service to ICE-SAR, the Icelandic lifeboat service. Renamed *Oddur V. Gíslason*, she was stationed at Grindavík.

▲ On trials shortly after being built.
(By courtesy of the RNLI)

▼ Poole: alongside at the RNLI Depot,
March 1999 (Nicholas Leach)

Newsbuoy

OFFICIAL NUMBER
1103

YEAR BUILT
1984

BUILDER
Halmatic Ltd hull, fit out by W. A. Souter, Cowes

YARD NO
—

WEIGHT
31 tons

COST
£394,226

DONOR
Special appeal by The Newspaper Society with various other appeals

STATIONS
Relief Fleet
23 Oct 1984 – 4 Jul 2004
(198/49)

DISPOSAL
Sold out of service in Jul 2005 to Faroe Islands, Nodoya Bajargingarfelag

In October 1983 another Arun was ordered for the Relief Fleet. The boat was fitted out at Souter Marine, in Cowes, between October 1983 and September 1984 and was named *Newsbuoy*. She had been funded by The Newspaper Society's special appeal, which had been organised from the Society's offices at Whitefriars House in London.

During her forty-hour trials, undertaken between 19 and 24 September 1984, *Newsbuoy* performed a service on passage to Weymouth. On 21 September she saved four people and the yacht *Nicola*. Another passage service took place on 24 September 1984, when the lifeboat assisted a cabin cruiser while returning to Poole.

Newsbuoy was named on 29 September 1984 on the Thames against the backdrop of Tower Bridge in the heart of London. The unusual setting of St Katharine Docks was crowded with onlookers and over 150 newsboys and girls from all over the country, who had been chosen to attend the ceremony as a reward for their part in raising money for the Local Newspaper Week lifeboat appeal.

During the ceremony T. D. Morris, president of The Newspaper Society, handed over the lifeboat to Vice-Admiral Sir Peter Compston, deputy chairman of the RNLI. The service of dedication was conducted by Prebendary Dewi Morgan, Rector of St Bride's Church, and Monsignor George Leonard. The Duke of Atholl, chairman of the RNLI Committee of Management and of the Westminster Press newspaper group, formally named the lifeboat *Newsbuoy*.

Newsbuoy's first relief duty was at Broughty Ferry which lasted for more than a year, from 28 November 1984 to 28 March 1986 and saw her launching thirteen times on service and saving one life. Her next duty was just a few days, at Stromness, and then from April to November 1986 she was at Portrush.

Newsbuoy remained in Scotland during the late 1980s, serving on relief at Stornoway and Aberdeen (1987), Buckie (1988) and Broughty Ferry (1988-89), Stornoway, Lerwick and Kirkwall (1989). Her time at Lerwick, between August and November, saw her undertake five launches, and included a particularly fine service. On 28 October 1989 she went to the fish factory ship *Azu*, of Nigeria, which was aground in Brei Wick Bay in near gale-force winds. The crew of thirty-three were evacuated and landed ashore at Lerwick. For this service the Thanks on Vellum was accorded to Coxswain/Mechanic Hewitt Clark and Vellum Service Certificates to the rest of the Lerwick crew.

Apart from a stint at Humber from February to March 1990, *Newsbuoy* was used exclusively at Scottish stations during the 1990s. She served at Aberdeen (1990), Stornoway, Stromness and Lochinver (1991), Kirkwall, Stromness and Thurso (1992), Mallaig, Islay and Stornoway (1993), Lochinver, Kirkwall and Stromness (1994), Campbeltown, Lerwick, Stromness, Aberdeen and Thurso (1995), Lerwick, Buckie and Stornoway (1996), Kirkwall, Aith and Lerwick (1997), Longhope (1998), and Troon and Mallaig (1999).

Her longest duty in the new century was a stint at Plymouth from 2002 to February 2003, and then she had a further year in the Relief Fleet before being taken out of service and put on the sale list in July 2004. In July 2005 she was sold out of service to the lifeboat service in the Faroe Islands and, renamed *Ziska*, became the Klaksvik lifeboat.

▲ Stornoway: on relief duty,
21 July 1989. (Tony Denton)

▼ Plymouth: on relief duty, August
2002. (Nicholas Leach)

Keith Anderson

OFFICIAL NUMBER
1106

YEAR BUILT
1985

BUILDER
Halmatic Ltd hull, fit out
by William Osborne Ltd,
Littlehampton

YARD NO
WO 2790

WEIGHT
30 tons 15 cwt

COST
£394,928

DONOR
Gift from Mrs Esme Anderson,
Grosvenor Square, London

STATIONS
Newhaven
9 Aug 1985 – Oct 1999
(521/119)
Relief Fleet
15 Nov 1999 – Oct 2000 (0/0)
Hartlepool
23 Oct 2000 – Aug 2003
(56/2)

DISPOSAL
Sold out of service in Jan 2006
to China Rescue & Salvage
Bureau

The lifeboat station at Newhaven in Sussex had been operating a 44ft Waveney class lifeboat for eight years when a new Arun lifeboat was sent to improve the station's capabilities. Newhaven was a key station on the Sussex coast and a mooring in the river was available.

The new boat was fitted out by William Osborne's during 1984 and into 1985, and between May and July 1985 was on trials out of Littlehampton, before being taken to the RNLI Depot at Poole. After crew training, she was sailed on an extended passage by her Newhaven crew back to station, arriving on 9 August 1985. Between 23 and 26 August she was in attendance at Portsmouth Navy Days, and on her return to Newhaven she was placed in service.

The boat was provided by a gift from Mrs Esme Anderson, of London, and was named *Keith Anderson* after the donor's husband. The naming ceremony took place at Newhaven on 27 May 1986, by when the lifeboat had launched thirty-three times on service and saved four lives. The branch president The Viscount Hampden welcomed the guests to the ceremony, and the lifeboat was officially presented to the RNLI by Mrs Anderson, who said that the occasion 'made her feel ten feet tall'. She also formally thanked her friend Lady Milner, of the Central London Ladies Lifeboat Committee, for suggesting that she might like to commemorate her husband by donating a lifeboat.

The Duke of Atholl, chairman of the RNLI, accepted the lifeboat and delivered her to the care of Newhaven. Mr G. W. Sargeant, branch chairman, accepted the lifeboat, and the Vicar of Staplefield, the Rev A. E. T. Hobbs, led the service of dedication. Mrs Anderson then named the lifeboat,

after which she and the official party boarded the boat for a brief demonstration and trip out to sea.

Keith Anderson served Newhaven with distinction, launching more than 500 times on service. Her most notable rescue took place on 16 October 1987 after the fishing boat *La François* was disabled during a hurricane. The lifeboat had to face force nine south-easterly winds, gusting to force eleven, as she left harbour. Although the fishing boat's crew could not speak English, a tow line was successfully rigged, and the boat was towed back to Newhaven through very rough seas. A framed letter of thanks was sent to Coxswain Leonard Patten for this service. The lifeboat was also involved in a long service on 4 April 1988, when she was at sea in a north-easterly gale for almost six and a half hours towing in the yacht *Aubric*, which had problems with her engine and sails.

After being replaced at Newhaven in November 1999, *Keith Anderson* was reallocated to the Relief Fleet and was initially taken to the RNLI Depot at Poole. However, she was then sent to Hartlepool as station boat, leaving Poole on 8 January and heading north via Newhaven, Ramsgate, Gorleston and Grimsby. Following a refit at Coastal Marine, Eyemouth, she was placed on station at Hartlepool on 23 October 2000, serving there for almost three years. She was then replaced and taken out of service.

After a period in storage at Poole, *Keith Anderson* was sold out of service in January 2006 to the China Rescue & Salvage Bureau. She was shipped from the UK on board a container ship, which departed Felixstowe on 19 February 2006. Once she had reached China, she was renamed *Huaying 395* and was one of three former Aruns based at Yan Tai.

▲ Newhaven: on exercise off the Sussex coast. (By courtesy of the RNLI)

▼ Hartlepool: leaving harbour on exercise, October 2001. (Nicholas Leach)

52-33

City of Belfast

OFFICIAL NUMBER
1107

YEAR BUILT
1985

BUILDER
Halmatic Ltd hull, fit out
by William Osborne Ltd,
Littlehampton

YARD NO
WO 2830

WEIGHT
31 tons 5 cwt

COST
£433,138

DONOR
The City of Belfast Appeal

STATIONS
Donaghadee
7 Dec 1985 – 19 Apr 2003
(322/58)
Relief Fleet
Apr 2003 – 2004 (14/0)

DISPOSAL
Sold out of service in Nov 2005
to China Rescue & Salvage
Bureau

▼ On trials before coming to
station. (By courtesy of the RNLI)

The important lifeboat station at Donaghadee covers Belfast Lough and had operated a Waveney class lifeboat since 1979, but in 1984 an Arun class lifeboat was allocated to the station. The hull was built by Halmatic in 1984 and the fitting out work was undertaken by William Osborne at Littlehampton in 1985.

In mid-November 1985 the Donaghadee crew went to the RNLI Depot at Poole to train on the new lifeboat before undertaking an extended passage back to station. This saw the lifeboat and her crew stop overnight at St Peter Port in the Channel Island on 24 November, after she had performed two services in the area, and then head to Newlyn harbour the following day.

After two days at Newlyn, where repairs to the port engine had to be completed, the lifeboat undertook an overnight crossing to Rosslare on 27 November, with an overnight stop at Wicklow the next day. On 29 November the lifeboat went north to Portpatrick, and the following day made the short trip across the North Channel to arrive in Donaghadee, where she was escorted to her new home by her predecessor, the 44ft Waveney *Arthur and Blanche Harris*. After two weeks of crew training, the lifeboat was placed on station on 7 December 1985, and she answered her first call just four days later.

Funded by a special appeal run in Northern Ireland, the new lifeboat was named *City of Belfast* in recognition of the generosity of the people of Belfast and Northern Ireland. The naming ceremony was held on 24 May 1986 in the harbour at Donaghadee with the chairman of the branch, Eric Reynolds, welcoming the guests to proceedings. Charles Neill, a Belfast harbour commissioner, formally presented *City of Belfast* to the RNLI on behalf of the patrons of the special appeal.

Vice-Admiral Sir Arthur Hezlet, a vice-president of the Institution, accepted the lifeboat and handed her into the care of Donaghadee station branch. Bill Sherrard, honorary secretary, accepted the lifeboat and, after the service of dedication conducted by local ministers, the Lord Mayor of Belfast, Alderman John Carson CBE, named the new lifeboat *City of Belfast*. On the deck of Ulster's newest lifeboat stood her crew, including Ruth Lennon, daughter of Coxswain Willie Lennon, preserving a family tradition of service going back four generations.

City of Belfast was well liked at Donaghadee and gave good service for eighteen years until being replaced by a new 14m Trent lifeboat in April 2003. She then served in the Relief Fleet for a year before being placed on the sale list. In November 2005 she was sold out of service to the China Rescue & Salvage Bureau, with a number of other Aruns, and was shipped to China in February 2006 from Felixstowe. In China, was renamed *Huaying 394* and was one of three boats based at Yan Tai.

▲ Donaghadee: returning to harbour after exercise, July 1995. (Nicholas Leach)

▼ Donaghadee: on exercise off the harbour, September 2002. (Nicholas Leach)

Margaret Russell Fraser

OFFICIAL NUMBER
1108

YEAR BUILT
1985

BUILDER
Halmatic Ltd hull, fit out by W.A. Souter, Cowes

YARD NO
—

WEIGHT
31 tons 5 cwt

COST
£417,616

DONOR
Bequest of Miss Margaret R. Fraser, Glasgow, together with other gifts and legacies

STATIONS
Relief Fleet
14 Jun 1986 – Apr 2002
(293/152)
Calshot
4 Apr 2002 – Aug 2004
(118/15)

DISPOSAL
Sold out of service in Dec 2004 to ICE-SAR Iceland

Another Arun was ordered for the Relief Fleet in 1984 bringing the number serving as relief boats to five. The latest one was fitted out at Souter Marine Ltd, Cowes, between August 1984 and November 1985. She undertook her self-righting trials on 19 November 1985, after which the electronic equipment was fitted. Her main trials programme was undertaken during January and February 1986, and in April 1986 she was handed over to the RNLI.

In April 1986 she was taken to the RNLI Depot at Poole, and on 10 May left for passage to London, arriving there on 12 May. She was berthed on the Thames at the Festival Pier Hall for two days, for the RNLI's Annual General Meeting, leaving London on 14 May to return to Poole. On 2 June 1986 she was taken north for her naming ceremony in Glasgow, calling at Holyhead on her way up the west coast. She arrived in Glasgow on 8 June, ready for the ceremony, which was held on 11 June 1986.

Glasgow was chosen because the funding for the new boat had come substantially from the legacy of a former resident of Glasgow, Miss Margaret Russell Fraser, after whom the lifeboat was named. The donor had requested that her bequest should benefit the RNLI in Scotland.

For the ceremony at the Yorkhill Basin, *Margaret Russell Fraser* had among her crew no fewer than four Scottish recipients of RNLI gallantry medals: Coxswain Alexander Gilchrist, Campbeltown (silver); Coxswain Ian Johnson, Troon (silver); Coxswain Mike Storey, Girvan (bronze); and crew member Arthur Hill of Largs (silver). The survey ship HMS *Hecate* provided the backdrop to the ceremony, which was opened by Cdr Cargill Sandeman.

Miss Mary Shanks, a personal friend of the deceased and an executor of her estate, formally handed the boat over to Lt Cdr Brian Miles, deputy director of the RNLI, and after a dedication of the boat Mrs Gray proceeded to the quayside and named the lifeboat *Margaret Russell Fraser*. The bottle broke, the crowd cheered and the boat manoeuvred alongside to take the platform party afloat for a short trip on the river Clyde.

The first relief duties undertaken by *Margaret Russell Fraser* were in Ireland, at Rosslare Harbour, Ballycotton and Valentia. She went to the Aran Islands in 1989, and in September 1989 began her first English relief duty at Yarmouth, staying until mid-November. While at Yarmouth she was involved in a fine service, on 28-29 October 1989 when she stood by the Maltese registered ro-ro cargo vessel *Al Kwather I*, which was at anchor three miles east-south-east of Peveril Point.

The vessel's cargo had shifted in the deteriorating weather conditions and *Margaret Russell Fraser* encountered very rough seas and heavy swell conditions during the passage to the casualty in south-westerly winds gusting to force eleven. Coxswain Kennett displayed exemplary boat-handling skills as he manoeuvred the lifeboat to rescue two of the eight crew from the casualty, and for this rescue he was awarded the bronze medal.

After sixteen years in the Relief Fleet, *Margaret Russell Fraser* was sent to Calshot as station lifeboat to replace the 33ft Brede in April 2002. She stayed at Calshot for a little over two years before being replaced by another Arun, 52-45 *Mabel Williams*, and she was then sold out of service in December 2004 to ICE-SAR, the Icelandic lifeboat and rescue service. Renamed *Ingibjörg*, she has been stationed at Höfn, on the country's south coast since 2005.

▲ Glasgow: naming and dedication
ceremony, 11 June 1986. (Tony Denton)

▼ Calshot: on exercise in the Solent,
April 2002. (Nicholas Leach)

52-35

City of Dublin

OFFICIAL NUMBER
1113

YEAR BUILT
1986

BUILDER
Halmatic Ltd hull, fit out by
Berthon Boat Co, Lymington

YARD NO
1013

WEIGHT
26 tons 5 cwt

COST
£543,552

DONOR
The City of Dublin Lifeboat
Appeal

STATIONS
Howth
22 Aug 1986 – Mar 2002
(260/63)
Relief Fleet
Mar 2002 – 7 Jul 2003
(25/0)

DISPOSAL
Sold out of service in Mar 2004
to ICE-SAR Iceland

In 1985 an Arun was allocated to Howth, the station which covered the north side of Dublin Bay, where the Watson lifeboat had been kept afloat in the harbour, and so a berth for the Arun was already in place. The new boat was fitted out at Berthon Boat Company, during the first six months of 1986 and undertook her initial trials in May that year.

Her final trials began on 22 May 1986 and lasted throughout June, at the end of which she left for the RNLI Depot at Poole. Training with the Howth crew was undertaken at the end of July and the new boat left Poole on 1 August 1986 for an extended passage to Howth. She arrived at her new station on 6 August and, after a further two weeks of training, was placed on service on 22 August.

Named *City of Dublin*, she was funded by the City of Dublin Lifeboat Appeal. A special committee, chaired by the Rt Hon Lord Mayor of Dublin, Alderman Bertie Ahern, TD, Minister for Labour, had been formed to fund half the cost of the new lifeboat and the Appeal raised more than £200,000. *City of Dublin* was named at Howth harbour on 16 May 1987 by the Lady Mayoress of Dublin.

A huge gathering of lifeboat supporters and branch and guild members attended the naming and dedication ceremony, despite the poor weather. John Guinness, chairman of Howth lifeboat station branch, opened proceedings and Harry Hannon, vice-chairman of the appeal executive committee, then formally delivered *City of Dublin* into the hands of Institution, and thanked everyone who had supported the appeal fund.

The Duke of Atholl accepted the lifeboat on behalf of the RNLI, and delivered it into the care of the Howth branch, saying: 'It is always pleasing to visit Ireland, where a warm and hospitable welcome is always assured. It is particularly pleasing to be present at such a significant occasion as this in Howth's lifeboat history'. Norman Wilkinson, honorary secretary, accepted the lifeboat and the service of dedication was led by the Most Rev Donald Caird, after which the Lady Mayoress, Mrs Miriam Ahern, named the new lifeboat.

City of Dublin served at Howth for sixteen years and undertook many services, the most notable of which took place on 16 November 1995, when the fishing vessel *Scarlet Buccaneer* went aground on the outer side of Howth East Pier breakwater and broke up in gale force winds and very rough seas. Attempts to effect a rescue using *City of Dublin* proved fruitless, so a team of lifeboatmen, in drysuits and life jackets, went along the breakwater to rescue the vessel's four crew from the land. All of them were safely recovered, but unfortunately one died while en route to hospital.

The Thanks Inscribed on Vellum was accorded to Second Coxswain/ Mechanic George Duffy in recognition of his leadership and courage during this service, and to Deputy Second Coxswain Ian Sheridan for his courage, endurance and personal initiative when, from the breakwater, he attempted to rescue the remaining survivor who was still clinging to the wreck after the other three had been washed overboard.

In March 2002 *City of Dublin* was replaced at Howth by a new 14m Trent class lifeboat and she was placed in the Relief Fleet for a further year, before being withdrawn from service and placed on the sale list. She was sold out of service in March 2004 to ICE-SAR, the Icelandic lifeboat service, and was renamed *Hafbjörg* for further service at Neskaupstaður on the east coast.

▲ On trials. (By courtesy of the RNLI)

▼ Howth: moored in the harbour, August 1995. (Nicholas Leach)

52-36

Roy and Barbara Harding

OFFICIAL NUMBER
1118

YEAR BUILT
1986

BUILDER
Halmatic Ltd hull, fit out
by William Osborne Ltd,
Littlehampton

YARD NO
WO 3010

WEIGHT
32 tons 5 cwt

COST
£466,448

DONOR
RNLI Funds, named in honour
of the late Captain Roy Harding
and his wife Barbara

STATIONS
Galway Bay/Aran Islands
4 Jul 1987 – 5 Jun 1997
(315/43)
Castletownbere
7 Apr 1998 – Jan 2004
(83/26)

DISPOSAL
Sold out of service in Jun 2004
to ICE-SAR Iceland

One of the three Aruns ordered during 1986 was allocated to the Galway Bay station on the west coast of Ireland. This busy station covers a large area, and the lifeboat was operated from a mooring at Kilronan on Inishmore, the largest of the Aran Islands. In 1995 the station was renamed Aran Islands. The new lifeboat was fitted out by William Osborne during 1986, with the trials programme starting on 16 February 1987, and self-righting trials took place on 27 February. After final trials in April 1987, by the end of the month the boat was ready.

Roy and Barbara Harding was named after Mrs Barbara Harding of Seaton, Devon, who had been honorary secretary of the Seaton, Beer and district branch since 1940, and her husband. Roy Harding was the RNLI's Operations Trials Officer during the initial development of the Arun class.

Roy and Barbara Harding's first duty saw her go to London's Festival Pier on the Thames on 11 May 1987 for the RNLI's Annual General Meeting the following day. After returning to Poole, she sailed at the end of May to La Coruna for the fifteenth International Lifeboat Conference, which was being hosted by Spain.

She sailed to Spain in company with the Norwegian lifeboat *Skomvaer III* and the Swedish lifeboat *Marjit Enjeullan*. The boats called at Roscoff, Belle Isle, Port Bloc, Santander, and Gijon, before reaching La Coruna on 1 June. *Roy and Barbara Harding* stayed in Spain until 6 June, playing her part at the conference, and then returned to British waters.

Training for the Aran Islands crew took place from 22 to 26 June, and she then went on an extended passage to her new station. After further crew training, she was placed on station on 4 July 1987. Her naming ceremony took place at Kilronan harbour on 11 June 1988. Mrs Barbara Harding had travelled from Devon and then been brought by the new Arun from Rossaveal to Kilronan. Lord Killanin, a member of the RNLI Committee of Management, delivered the lifeboat to the Galway Bay branch. The service of dedication was conducted by the Rt Rev John Neill, and the Very Rev Athair Padraic O. Tuairisg, and at the end of the ceremony, Mrs Harding christened the new lifeboat.

Roy and Barbara Harding served at Aran Islands for ten years, launching over 300 times, often providing an ambulance service to the mainland. Her most noteworthy service came on 14 August 1989 when she was involved in saving two skin divers in winds up to force ten. The lifeboat's Y class inflatable had to be used to reach the divers, despite the severe conditions. Following the service, Coxswain Padraig Dillane and crew members Seamus Flaherty and Martin Fitzpatrick were accorded the Thanks Inscribed on Vellum.

Roy and Barbara Harding was replaced at Aran Islands in June 1997, and was then reallocated to Castletownbere, a new station in south-west Ireland. After a survey at Falmouth in 1996, she was refitted at Appledore in early 1997 ready for her new station. Extensive training by the Castletownbere crew took place during early 1998 and on 7 April she become the station's first lifeboat.

After leaving Castletownbere in January 2004, *Roy and Barbara Harding* was taken to the RNLI Depot at Poole. She was sold out of service in June 2004 to Iceland's lifeboat service, ICE-SAR, and in October 2004 was taken to Iceland. She was renamed *Gunnbjörg* and stationed at Raufarhöfn.

▲ On trials before going to Galway Bay.
(By courtesy of the RNLI)

▼ Castletownbere: returning to station after
exercise, August 2003. (Nicholas Leach)

Kenneth Thelwall

OFFICIAL NUMBER
1123

YEAR BUILT
197

BUILDER
Halmatic Ltd hull, fit out by
Berthon Boat Co, Lymington

YARD NO
1014

WEIGHT
30 tons 6 cwt

COST
£574,433

DONOR
Legacy of Mr Kenneth Thelwall,
Walkington, Yorkshire

STATIONS
Humber
13 Aug 1987 – Mar 1997
(383/68)
Relief Fleet
Mar 1997 – Sep 1998 (28/10)
Holyhead
17 Sep 1998 – Dec 2003
(101/15)

DISPOSAL
Sold out of service in Jul 2005
to China Rescue & Salvage
Bureau

After ten years of service at the busy Humber station at Spurn Point, the seventh Arun lifeboat to be built, *City of Bradford IV*, was replaced by a new 52ft version of the class. Named *Kenneth Thelwall*, the new boat was fitted out by Berthon Boat Co at Lymington between June 1986 and July 1987. Her builder's trials were undertaken between May and July 1987, with final trials being completed on 10 July 1987.

She reached the RNLI Depot at Poole on 19 July 1987, and between 3 and 10 August the Humber lifeboat crew undertook training on their new boat. She left Poole on 10 August and travelled north to the Humber, arriving three days later and immediately being placed on station.

The new lifeboat was named on 19 September 1987 at Hull Marina in front of a large crowd of supporters. Christopher Hobson, executor of the estate of Kenneth Thelwall, handed the boat over to the RNLI and the Rev Frank La Touche, port chaplain to the Mission to Seamen, conducted the service of dedication. Commander Brian Miles, RNLI Deputy Director, paid tribute to the most loyal group of lifeboat supporters, lifeboatmen's wives, and then introduced Mrs Ann Bevan, wife of Superintendent Coxswain Brian Bevan, who formally named the lifeboat *Kenneth Thelwall*.

Kenneth Thelwall spent ten years on station at the Humber, and during that time launched almost 400 times on service. She performed many difficult services, including one on 17 September 1989 when, manned by her full-time crew, she saved sixteen men from the blazing tanker *Philips Oklahoma*. The tanker had collided with the bulk carrier *Fiona*, and one of her tanks had been ruptured. Following this service, a letter of thanks from

the Philippine Ambassador Thomas Syquia, on behalf of the Philippine Government and people, was sent to the Humber crew for their efforts.

Kenneth Thelwall was replaced at the Humber in March 1997 by a new 17m Severn class lifeboat, after which she was used as a Relief lifeboat until September 1998. During her eighteen months in the Relief Fleet she went back to Humber on a number of occasions until October 1997, being stored at Legget's yard at Grimsby when not needed at Spurn Point. She then went to Hartlepool (December 1997), and in 1998 served at Tynemouth (January), Hartlepool (February to March), Barry Dock (March to June) before going to Dickie's boatyard at Bangor for a refit which lasted from 22 June to 7 September 1998.

By then, she had been reallocated to Holyhead and, after the refit, a short training passage was arranged with her new crew, going from Conwy to Douglas overnight on 14 September before reaching Holyhead the following day. With further crew training completed, she was placed on station at Holyhead on 17 September 1998.

Kenneth Thelwall served at Holyhead until December 2003, launching more than 100 times on service, until being replaced by another new 17m Severn. She then went to the RNLI Depot at Poole to be placed on the sale list in January 2004. She remained in storage at Poole for more than a year before a sale was agreed and she became one of a number of Aruns to go to the China Rescue & Salvage Bureau. She left the UK for the last time on 5 August 2005, on board COSCO container ship *Cosco Rotterdam* out of Felixstowe, and was taken to China, where she was renamed *Huaying 399* and based at Wenzhou, Zhejiang.

▲ Humber: moored off the Pilot Jetty at
Spurn Point, 1994. (Nicholas Leach)

▼ Holyhead: on exercise off the Anglesey coast,
June 2003. (Nicholas Leach)

City of Glasgow III

OFFICIAL NUMBER
1134

YEAR BUILT
1987

BUILDER
Halmatic Ltd hull, fit out by W. A. Souter, Cowes

YARD NO
0002

WEIGHT
30 tons 8 cwt

COST
£562,248

DONOR
The City of Glasgow Lifeboat Appeal, together with other gifts and legacies

STATIONS
Troon
25 Oct 1987 – Feb 2004
(432/139)
Relief Fleet
Feb 2004 – Jul 2005 (0/0)

DISPOSAL
Sold out of service in Nov 2005 to ICE-SAR Iceland

Troon lifeboat station, covering the entrance to the Clyde, had been operating 44ft Waveney class lifeboats for almost twenty years when, in 1986, a new 52ft Arun was allocated to the station to upgrade its capabilities. The boat was fitted out by Souter Marine at Cowes, Isle of Wight, between October 1986 and June 1987.

Between June and August 1987 the Arun undertook trials out of Cowes before being taken to the RNLI Depot at Poole at the end of August to complete her forty-hour trials. From 25 September the Troon crew, led by Coxswain Ian Johnston, undertook training on the new boat out of Poole, until 2 October, when they left the south coast and headed north. The lifeboat arrived at Troon on 7 October following an extended passage, and, after further crew training undertaken during October, was placed on station on 25 October.

Named *City of Glasgow III*, the boat was funded by the City of Glasgow Lifeboat Appeal, led by The Lord Provost of Glasgow, and was named at a ceremony at Troon on 16 April 1988 in front of many of those who had contributed to the appeal. With the branch chairman Tom Wyllie in the chair, and the Lord Provost of Glasgow representing the donors, tributes were paid to everyone associated with the fund-raising efforts.

His Grace the Duke of Atholl delivered the boat into the care of the station, and she was accepted by Jimmy Manson, honorary secretary. Following a vote of thanks from the guild president Catherine Fraser, the Rev Webster conducted the service of dedication. At the end of the formalities, the Lady Provost of Glasgow, Mrs Gray, pressed the button to release the champagne over the bow of the lifeboat. The engines were then started and the boat picked up the platform party and guests to take them for a short trip to sea.

During her time at Troon, *City of Glasgow III* was involved in a couple of notable services, with the small Y class inflatable she carried proving invaluable. On 14 July 1988 she went to the aid of the Ayr Sea Cadets whose 30ft vessel was ashore just south of Ayr harbour. Once on scene, the lifeboat launched its Y boat, which was taken through very turbulent surf over rocks. The boat then ferried seven children, all girls aged fourteen or under, and one adult back to the lifeboat, which took them to Ayr. For this service, the Thanks Inscribed on Vellum was accorded to David Seaward and Paul Aspin who manned the Y boat. Coxswain/Mechanic Ian Johnson received a framed letter of appreciation from the Duke of Atholl.

Another fine service was performed on 23 May 1992 when *City of Glasgow III* rescued the four crew from the yacht *Anat* and saved the boat. The yacht, with two men and two teenage boys on board, had suffered steering and engine failure in winds gusting to gale force and rough seas three miles east of Holy Isle. A framed letter of appreciation was presented to Coxswain Ian Johnson and his crew in recognition of the fine teamwork shown during this service.

In February 2004 *City of Glasgow III* was replaced at Troon by a new 14m Trent lifeboat, and she was taken to the RNLI Depot at Poole as a Relief lifeboat. After little more than a year, on 4 July 2005, she was placed on the sale list, and was sold out of service in November 2005 to ICE-SAR, the Icelandic lifeboat service. She was shipped to Iceland in January 2006, renamed *Sveinbjörn Sveinsson*, and placed on station at Vopnafjörður.

▲ On a courtesy visit to Glasgow,
24 October 1987. (Tony Denton)

▼ Troon: on exercise off the harbour with Coxswain Ian
Johnson at the helm, July 1995. (Nicholas Leach)

Mickie Salvesen

OFFICIAL NUMBER
1135

YEAR BUILT
1988

BUILDER
Halmatic Ltd, Havant

YARD NO
WR8722

WEIGHT
31 tons

COST
£587,133

DONOR
Bequest of the late Mrs Mary
'Mickie' Salvesen

STATIONS
Kirkwall
5 Jul 1988 – Mar 1998
(89/35)
Relief Fleet
Mar 1998 – Aug 1998 (1/0)
Aberdeen
13 Aug 1998 – Jul 2000
(25/0)
Relief Fleet
Jul 2000 – Aug 2003 (29/9)
Barry Dock
8 Aug 2003 – Jan 2006 (57/0)

DISPOSAL
Sold out of service in 2006 to
ICE-SAR Iceland

In the 1980s, as the RNLI was looking to replace the large 70ft Clyde class lifeboats, the Arun was deemed to be the ideal replacement for the Clyde at Kirkwall in Orkney, *Grace Paterson Ritchie*. While the large Clyde boats, conceived as rescue cruisers in the 1960s, had their advantages, speed was not one of them and the Arun was much faster. The Arun allocated to Kirkwall, *Mickie Salvesen*, was fitted out by Halmatic at Havant between November 1986 and January 1988.

The boat underwent builder's trials during the first few months of 1988, reaching the RNLI Depot at Poole in April 1988 ready for service. Training for the Kirkwall crew took place during mid-June and on 18 June *Mickie Salvesen* left Poole for Orkney. She reached Kirkwall a week later and on 5 July she was placed on station.

Funded from the bequest of the late Mrs Mary 'Mickie' Salvesen, the new lifeboat was named after her donor, who also provided the 47ft Tyne lifeboat *Norman Salvesen* for Wick. The naming ceremony of the Arun took place on 20 August 1988 at Kirkwall's old harbour, with members of the donor's family in attendance. Historic links with Norway were maintained by the presence of the Norwegian lifeboat *Dagfinn Paust* at the ceremony and Admiral Steimler, of the Norwegian Lifeboat Society.

Sir Charles McGrigor, Convener of the Scottish Lifeboat Council, formally handed over the lifeboat to honorary secretary Captain Bill Spence during the ceremony, and after the service of dedication led by the Rev Cant, Minister of St Magnus Cathedral, Mrs Doris Sutcliffe named the boat in memory of her late sister.

Mickie Salvesen served for a decade in Orkney, and she was involved in a fine medal-winning service on 13 September 1998, having been on station for just six weeks. She went to the bulk cement carrier *BC Mercurius*, with six persons on board, which had suffered engine failure in gale force winds. The Coastguard helicopter from Sumburgh winched four crew off, but the master and chief engineer remained on board to save the ship, getting the lifeboat to tow her.

Despite the difficult conditions, with the coaster rolling violently, the lifeboat was manoeuvred close enough for a line to be passed across on the first attempt. She then managed to tow the vessel clear of the rocks and although the tow rope parted three times, the lifeboat crew rapidly secured it each time. When the casualty was 800 yards offshore, the vessel was anchored and *Mickie Salvesen* stood by until the tug *Kintore* arrived to make fast a tow line. For his outstanding seamanship during this arduous service, Captain Sinclair was awarded the bronze medal.

Mickie Salvesen served at Kirkwall until 1998, when she was replaced by a 17m Severn lifeboat, after which she was reallocated to the Relief Fleet. She served on Relief at Lochinver in April 1998 and Islay in May and June 1998 before going to Buckie Boatyard for overhaul ready for station duties at Aberdeen in August 1998. She stayed for two years at Aberdeen before being replaced by another new 17m Severn and then going back into the Relief Fleet in July 2000 for three years .

In August 2003 she was reallocated to Barry Dock, where she served until January 2006. She was then sold out of service to ICE-SAR for further life-saving service in Iceland and left Poole in early September 2006 for her new home. She was stationed at Patreksfjörður on Iceland's west coast, a station founded in 2004, and was renamed *Vörður II*.

▲ On trials before entering service.
(By courtesy of the RNLI)

▼ Kirkwall: moored alongside the West Pier,
August 1997. (Nicholas Leach)

52-40

City of Plymouth

OFFICIAL NUMBER
1136

YEAR BUILT
1987

BUILDER
Halmatic Ltd hull, fit out by W. A.
Souter, Cowes

YARD NO
0007

WEIGHT
29 tons 3 cwt

COST
£592,478

DONOR
The City of Plymouth Appeal
with other gifts and legacies

STATIONS
Plymouth
26 Jan 1988 – 1 Nov 2002
(579/115)
Relief Fleet
Nov 2002 – Sep 2004 (4/0)

DISPOSAL
Sold out of service in Oct 2004
to ICE-SAR Iceland

Having been served by a 44ft Waveney class lifeboat since 1974, Plymouth lifeboat station was allocated an Arun lifeboat in 1986. After the hull had been completed by Halmatic during 1986, it was taken to Souter marine at Cowes for fitting out during 1987. By December 1987 the fit out was largely complete and the first trials were undertaken, and on 19 December the boat arrived at Poole after her forty-hour trials.

Crew training for the Plymouth crew took place in January 1988, and on 15 January the new lifeboat left for her station. She arrived at Plymouth on 17 January after an extended training passage and, following further crew training and familiarisation, was placed on station on 26 January 1988. She answered her first call that evening, towing in a Looe fishing vessel which was drifting without power in heavy seas off Rame Head.

The lifeboat had been funded by a local appeal in Plymouth, which had raised over £130,000, and this had been supplemented by bequests from George Wilfred Glass, Phyllis Maud Lyneham, Margaret Scott, Dorothy Janet Gertrude Singleton and various other gifts and legacies. In recognition of the main source of funding, she was named *City of Plymouth*.

The naming ceremony of *City of Plymouth* took place on 15 April 1988 at The Parade, Sutton Harbour in Plymouth in sea mist and damp weather. The branch chairman, Duncan Godefroy, welcomed guests from the city and neighbouring lifeboat stations and patron of the fund, Lord Mayor of Plymouth Councillor Tony Parish, formally handed over the lifeboat to Raymond Cory, deputy chairman of the RNLI. Major Philip Reed, honorary secretary, accepted the new boat and a service of dedication was

conducted by the station's honorary chaplain, Derek Tidball; , the lesson was read by crew member Dr Steve Ray. Following the blessing, Vice Admiral Sir Robert Gerkin, president of the station and chairman of the appeal, invited the Lady Mayoress to name the lifeboat *City of Plymouth*.

City of Plymouth had an operational career of just sixteen years with the RNLI, fourteen of which were spent at Plymouth. However, despite a relatively short career at her Devon station, she gained an outstanding service record, launching 579 times.

One of the more notable rescues in which *City of Plymouth* was involved took place on 6 September 1995 after the Lowestoft fishing vessel *Senex Fidelis* got into difficulty off Rame Head in heavy seas. When the lifeboat reached the casualty, conditions had deteriorated with a severe gale force nine wind gusting to storm force ten. The fishing vessel was being pushed towards the headland, but the lifeboat crew managed to pass a line across at the first attempt and were then able to bring the vessel to safety. For this rescue, in which the fishing vessel and its five crew were rescued, the Thanks Inscribed on Vellum was accorded to Coxswain Patrick Marshall.

In November 2002 *City of Plymouth* left Plymouth for refit and did not return, as a new 17m Severn lifeboat was sent to the station the following year. So she was reallocated to the Relief Fleet and spent almost two years as a Relief lifeboat. She was withdrawn from service in September 2004 and a month later was sold to ICE-SAR, the Icelandic lifeboat service. She was shipped to Iceland at the end of 2004 and in early 2005, having been renamed *Hunabjörg*, was placed on station at Skagastrond, a small port on the country's north coast.

▲ Plymouth: moored in Millbay Marina, May 1997. (Nicholas Leach)

▼ Plymouth: arriving at the small harbour of Looe during a joint exercise with Fowey lifeboat, April 2002. (Paul Richards)

52-41

Ann Lewis Fraser

OFFICIAL NUMBER
1143

YEAR BUILT
1988

BUILDER
Halmatic Ltd hull, fit out by
Berthon Boat Co, Lymington

YARD NO
1014

WEIGHT
31 tons

COST
£552,162

DONOR
Gift from the Hugh Fraser
Foundation

STATIONS
Barra Island
22 Jul 1988 – Mar 1998
(103/44)
Tobermory
5 Jul 1998 – 20 Aug 2003
(103/4)
Relief Fleet
Aug 2003 – 4 Jul 2005 (8/0)

DISPOSAL
Sold out of service in 2005
to China Rescue & Salvage
Bureau

▼ At RNLI Depot, Poole, April
1988, during crew training.
(Nicholas Leach)

Two Aruns were completed in 1988 and both were allocated to stations on Scotland's west coast. The first was sent to Barra Island, at the southern tip of the Western Isles, where the small community at Castlebay was home of the lifeboat, and the second, 52-42 Murray Lornie, went to Lochinver on the mainland.

The Barra boat was built at Halmatic during the winter of 1986-87 and it was then taken to Lymington for fitting out by Berthon Boat Co. The forty-hour trials took place between 25 and 30 April 1988, after which the boat was sent to the RNLI Depot at Poole ready for crew training during May 1988. The Barra Island crew undertook an extended passage to take their new boat home, leaving Poole on 27 May and arriving at Barra on 1 June 1988.

The new lifeboat was funded by the Hugh Fraser Foundation and named *Ann Lewis Fraser* at a ceremony on 7 September 1988 held in the early evening. In the shelter of the pier and overlooked by Kismul Castle, Father MacLellan, chairman of the branch, opened the proceedings. Dr K. G. Chrystie, representing the trustees of the Hugh Fraser Foundation, paid tribute to the late Hugh Fraser and

his sister, who instigated the gift, and formally handed the boat over to Sir Charles McGrigor, convener of the Scottish Lifeboat Council, who in turn passed the lifeboat into the care of the Barra Island branch. The service of dedication was conducted by Father MacLellan, after which Mrs Mary Chrystie named the lifeboat.

Ann Lewis Fraser served at Barra Island for a decade before she was replaced by a new 17m Severn. She left the Outer Hebrides in March 1998 and was reallocated to Tobermory. Before going to her new station, she was taken to Nobles Boatyard at Girvan for a refit, which lasted from March to June 1998. She left Girvan on 27 June and undertook a training passage with her new crew, stopping overnight at Port St Mary and Portrush. She arrived at Tobermory on 29 June 1988 and, after a further training passage, was placed on station on 5 July.

Ann Lewis Fraser spent just over five years at Tobermory. During her time at the station, she was damaged when, in December 1998, she hit an underwater object while en route to search for four missing persons in the Sound of Iona. Following the incident, she was immediately towed to Silvers Boatyard at Rosneath, via Campbeltown, by the Relief Arun *Duchess of Kent*. The hull and engine repairs took almost a year, and she did not return to station at Tobermory until 12 November 1999.

In August 2003 *Ann Lewis Fraser* left Tobermory and was reallocated to the Relief Fleet and served as a Relief lifeboat for a further two years, until July 2005. She was then sold to the China Rescue & Salvage Bureau, being shipped to China in April 2006. Following the passage east as deck cargo on a container ship, she was renamed *Huaying 392* and stationed at Shantou, Nanhai Rescue Bureau.

▲ Barra Island: at moorings in Castlebay, April 1996. (Gary Markham)

▼ Tobermory: leaving harbour, August 2003. (Nicholas Leach)

52-42

Murray Lornie

OFFICIAL NUMBER
1144

YEAR BUILT
1988

BUILDER
Halmatic Ltd hull, fit out by
Robson, South Shields

YARD NO
—

WEIGHT
31 tons

COST
£553,417

DONOR
Trustees of the Ben Vorlich
Trust, based in Jersey, with the
bequest of Miss Elsie Agnes
Grierson and other gifts

STATIONS
Lochinver
20 Jul 1989 – Nov 2003
(144/64)
Castletownbere
30 Jan 2004 – Aug 2004
(18/0)
Relief Fleet
2004 – 5 Jul 2005 (17/0)

DISPOSAL
Sold out of service in 2005 to
ICE-SAR Iceland

▼ At RNLI Depot, Poole on 14
April 1989 prior to going on
station. (Nicholas Leach)

Along with the Arun allocated to Barra Island, another was ordered at the same time for the station at Lochinver, a remote but busy fishing port in the far north-west of Scotland. Funded by trustees of the Ben Vorlich Trust, based in Jersey, with the bequest of Miss Elsie Agnes Grierson and other gifts, the new boat was named *Murray Lornie*.

The boat was built at Halmatic and fitted out at Robson's Boatyard, South Shields. The initial trials programme, including the self-righting trials, was completed during early September 1988 with the main trials completed by the end of October. Following her completion, *Murray Lornie* was taken on an extended passage to Poole between 12 and 16 December, which included her forty-hour trials.

At the time of her building, the RNLI was looking at a new design of fast afloat lifeboat to replace the Arun, and used *Murray Lornie* as a test bed for more powerful engines which could be used in a faster boat. After further trials out of Poole had been undertaken between December 1988 and early January 1989, she was therefore taken to Berthon Boat Co at Lymington on 5 January for her main engines to be uprated. She returned to Poole on 20

January, and for the next three months was involved in a series of evaluation trials with the new engines.

The new lifeboat was named at a ceremony on 25 August 1989, when a large number of supporters, including some from the Channel Islands who had been associated with the funding of the new boat, gathered at Lochinver. The whole community was involved in the occasion, which began with a lone piper leading the platform party. The chairman of Lochinver branch, Alex Strachan, opened the proceedings and Richard Falle, representing the Ben Vorlich Trust, formally delivered the boat to the RNLI.

Sir Charles McGrigor accepted her and in turn passed her into the care of the station honorary secretary, Captain Campbell. The service of dedication was conducted by the Rev Hurst, assisted by the Rev Tamata. Maurice Thomas, a son of the donor, spoke briefly before releasing the champagne bottle over the bow of the lifeboat. The lifeboat then took the invited guests for a short trip afloat.

Murray Lornie gave good service at Lochinver for just over fourteen years, during which time the majority of her services were to help fishing vessels. She was replaced at Lochinver in November 2003, after which she was reallocated to Castletownbere, arriving at her new south-west Ireland home on 30 January 2004. However, she stayed there for only a few months and in August 2004 was replaced by a new 17m Severn class lifeboat.

In July 2005 she was placed on the sale list and was sold out of service to ICE-SAR, the Icelandic lifeboat service. She was shipped to Iceland in January 2006 and was placed on station at Siglufjörður, on the northern coast of the country, where she entered service renamed *Sigurvin*.

▲ Lochinver: moored alongside,
July 1995. (Nicholas Leach)

▼ Castletownbere: putting out on exercise,
April 2005. (Nicholas Leach)

52-43

The Queen Mother

Following the success of the trials with 54ft Arun *City of Bradford IV* at Thurso, the station was allocated a new Arun, which was ordered in 1988 and fitted out by William Osborne at Littlehampton. The initial trials began at the end of September 1988, with the main trials lasting from 24 October to 21 November 1988. Final trials took place in early January 1989 and, after the completion of forty-hour trials in February, the new lifeboat was taken to Poole.

Crew training was undertaken out of Poole in mid-March 1989 and on 18 March the boat left Poole and headed north on the long passage to her station. She reached her new base at Scrabster harbour on 24 March and was placed on station at 7pm that day. The cost of the lifeboat had been met from the bequest of Miss Sarah Sinclair Gray and the Institution's funds, and the boat was named *The Queen Mother* in honour of HM Queen Elizabeth The Queen Mother, who had granted her approval to the name.

The naming ceremony was held at Scrabster on 9 August 1989, with Her Majesty, the guest of honour, being welcomed by Hugh Shaw, chairman of Thurso branch. Michael Vernon, chairman of the RNLI, delivered the lifeboat into the care of Thurso station, on whose behalf she was accepted by Mr George Gibson, the station's honorary secretary.

Following the service of dedication led by the Rev Johnstone, Her Majesty named the lifeboat. With a tribute to lifeboat crews, their wives and all voluntary supporters, the Queen Mother pressed the button, the bottle dropped to the foredeck of the lifeboat, and three cheers echoed around Scrabster. The lifeboat then took the guests for a short trip in the choppy seas of the Pentland Firth.

The Queen Mother served at Thurso for fifteen years and undertook a number of difficult rescues. On 15 September 1997 she launched to the fishing vessel *Aztec*, with four crew, which was in difficulties in gale force winds. In rough seas, the lifeboat battled to reach the casualty, maintaining a speed of fourteen knots despite the storm force ten winds.

Another fishing vessel, *Vigilant*, had taken *Aztec* in tow and so *The Queen Mother* escorted the vessels towards Thurso. But off Holborn Head, the line parted leaving *Aztec* adrift. In seas up to 35ft high, the lifeboat crew successfully passed across a towline and, at 6.25pm, the lifeboat brought the fishing vessel clear of the headland, despite having only one engine working. For this service, Second Coxswain William Munroe was accorded the Thanks on Vellum.

The Queen Mother was replaced at Thurso in April 2004 by a new 17m Severn, and then went to Buckie Boatyard, having been reallocated to Longhope. She served at Longhope for two years, during which time she was involved in a difficult service to the yacht *Dasher*, from which three people were saved, a service for which Coxswain Kevin Kirkpatrick was accorded the Thanks on Vellum.

When she was withdrawn in January 2009, *The Queen Mother* had the distinction of being the last Arun in operational service with the RNLI. She was taken to the RNLI Depot at Poole and placed on the sale list the following month, being subsequently sold to the Montevideo Pilot Association. On 4 June 2009 she passed through Dover en route to Gravesend, from where she went to Felixstowe for shipping to Montevideo. She arrived in Uruguay in July 1999 and, renamed *Ederra 4*, took up her duties as a pilot boat.

▲ Thurso: on exercise off Scrabster, August 1997. (Nicholas Leach)

▼ Longhope: on exercise off Hoy having just taken over as station lifeboat, June 2004 (Nicholas Leach)

Hibernia

OFFICIAL NUMBER
1150

YEAR BUILT
1988

BUILDER
Halmatic Ltd hull, fit out
by William Osborne Ltd,
Littlehampton

YARD NO
WO 3200

WEIGHT
29 tons 18 cwt

COST
£577,826

DONOR
The Irish Government from
monies provided for in the
Irish Sailors and Soldiers
Land Trust Act 1988

STATIONS
Relief Fleet
16 Sep 1989 – 7 Mar 2007
(315/44)

DISPOSAL
Sold out of service in 2007
to China Rescue & Salvage
Bureau

One of the last Aruns to be built, as the build programme neared its end, was *Hibernia*. She was funded by the Irish Government from monies provided for in the Irish Sailors and Soldiers Land Trust Act 1988, and was allocated to the Relief Fleet. Ordered in 1987, she was fitted out by William Osborne between June 1988 and June 1989, with self-righting trials in March 1989, her main trials the following month, and her final trials programme from 6 to 21 June 1989.

After her forty-hour trials at the end of June 1989, she was taken to the RNLI Depot at Poole during July and August, when further trials were undertaken, and on 21 August she left for Arklow, on Ireland's east coast, where she arrived three days later. She had a quick paint-up at Tyrell's yard in Arklow in preparation for her naming, before heading to Dublin bay on 15 September for the ceremony at Howth the following day.

The naming ceremony was held at Howth Harbour, with Mrs Maureen Haughey christening the new lifeboat *Hibernia* after she had been formally handed over to the chairman of the RNLI, Michael Vernon, by An Taoiseach (Prime Minister of Ireland) Charles Haughey. The blessing and dedication ceremony was conducted by The Most Rev Donald Caird DD, the Right Rev Monsignor Richard Maher, Rev Paul Kingston and Rev Dr William O'Neill. The RNLI's Director, Lt Cdr Brian Miles, was also in attendance.

On handing over the new lifeboat, Mr Haughey praised the work of the RNLI in Ireland and thanked the volunteer lifeboat crews who served the stations round the country, saying: 'They give selflessly of their time and are totally committed, we owe them a great debt of thanks for the most valuable work they perform'.

Having been funded from Irish sources, the boat served mainly at Irish stations, taking up her first Relief duty at Donaghadee on 23 September 1989, a few days after her naming. She stayed at Donaghadee until 15 December 1989 and then went back to Howth, where she stood in for *City of Dublin* until May 1990.

She went on to undertake Relief duties at Rosslare Harbour (1990), Aran Islands (1991), Ballyglass (1991-92), Ballycotton (1992-93), Portrush (1993), Valentia (1994), before coming to her first Welsh station, Fishguard, in November 1994. She also served at Fenit (1995-96) before going to the Welsh stations of Barry Dock (1996 and 1998) and Holyhead (1998). She was at Castletownbere in 1998 and Howth, Barra and Portrush in 1999. Her first English duty was at Torbay from June to July 1999, and she was also at Weymouth, before returning to Ireland for a stint at Valentia.

In October 2000, while serving at the Aran Islands on the west coast, *Hibernia* was involved in a fine service. She launched three times, on 3, 4 and 5 October, to search for the survivors of a sunken Spanish trawler, with her crew spending a total of thirty hours at sea in gale force winds. Second Coxswain Patrick Mullen was accorded the Thanks on Vellum for this service.

Hibernia spent seventeen years in the Relief Fleet, launching more than 300 times on service. She was taken out of service in March 2007 and later that year was sold to the China Salvage and Rescue Bureau. In mid-July 2007 she went to Felixstowe port to be loaded onto a container ship bound for China. The ship took a month to get to Hong Kong, where the Arun was unloaded and taken to her new station at the Waigaoqiao Base, Donghai Bureau, after being renamed *Huaying 390*.

▲ Off the coast of Northern Ireland.
(Colin Watson)

▼ Barry Dock: setting out while on relief,
November 2005. (Nicholas Leach)

52-45

Mabel Williams

OFFICIAL NUMBER
1159

YEAR BUILT
1990

BUILDER
Halmatic Ltd hull, fit out by
Robson, South Shields

YARD NO
—

WEIGHT
31 tons 10 cwt

COST
£640,001

DONOR
Bequest of Mrs Mabel Williams

STATIONS
Ballyglass
29 Aug 1990 – Aug 1998
(52/19)
Relief Fleet
Aug 1998 – 2001 (54/2)
Rosslare Harbour
9 Sep 2001 – Jun 2004 (28/19)
Calshot
27 Aug 2004 – Feb 2007
(115/0)

DISPOSAL
Sold out of service in 2007 to
China Rescue & Salvage Bureau

The penultimate Arun to be built was destined for Ballyglass, in Co Mayo. This had become the first new offshore lifeboat station to be opened on the west coast of Ireland since 1927 when it was established in 1989 with the 54ft Arun *City of Bradford IV.* The hull of the forty-fifth Arun was moulded by Halmatic and fitted out at Robson's boatyard at South Shields, on the river Tyne, one of only two Aruns fitted out there.

The hull went to South Shields in October 1989 and by March 1990 was ready for the passage south, having completed her main trials. Her final trials were completed during January and February 1990, and on 9 March she reached the RNLI Depot at Poole. During early June 1990 the Ballyglass crew were in Poole for crew training on their new boat, and she left Poole on 8 June for an extended eight-day training passage to Ballyglass.

She was at Ballyglass for three days before a further training passage was undertaken to Kilronan, and then she went to Valentia Marine for repairs to her engines. She eventually returned to Ballyglass on 25 August and was placed on station four days later.

The lifeboat was funded from the bequest of Mrs Mabel Williams together with the RNLI's funds, and she was named *Mabel Williams* on 4 May 1991 at Ballyglass Pier by Mrs Mary Robinson, President of Ireland. The service of dedication and blessing was conducted by the Most Rev Thomas Finnegan, Bishop of Killala and the Right Rev John Neill, Bishop of Tuam, Killala and Achonry.

Handing over the new lifeboat to the Ballyglass branch, the RNLI chairman, Michael Vernon, said the ceremony was the culmination of several years of intensive study by the RNLI after the necessity for a lifeboat station on the

Mayo coast, between Galway Bay and Arranmore lifeboat stations, had been established. Paddy Leech, honorary secretary of Ballyglass branch, accepted the lifeboat and Mrs Robinson, who praised the voluntary work done by lifeboat crews, named the boat.

Mabel Williams served at Ballyglass for only eight years before being replaced by a new 17m Severn lifeboat. She was then reallocated to the Relief Fleet, spending a few days on Relief at Achill Island after leaving Ballyglass in August 1998, before heading south. She had various other duties in Ireland, including at Howth (1998), Fenit, Castletownbere and Aran Islands (all 1999), and Fenit again in 2000.

Then, rather unexpectedly, she went to Rosslare Harbour on 9 September 2001 after their Arun, 52-26 *St Brendan*, was damaged beyond repair after being hit by one of the Stena Line ferries that operate to Wales. She was subsequently officially placed on station at Rosslare Harbour, and served there until June 2004, undertaking some fine rescues.

When a new 17m Severn arrived at Rosslare, after a new berth had been constructed, *Mabel Williams* was reallocated to Calshot, where she replaced another Arun (52-34). She served at Calshot until February 2007, by when the RNLI was withdrawing the last few Aruns from service. After being replaced by the 47ft Tyne *Sarah Emily Harrop* at Calshot, she was taken to the RNLI Depot at Poole and placed on the sale list.

She was sold to the China Rescue & Salvage Bureau in spring 2007 and on 18 July was taken by container ship from Felixstowe to China, with the voyage to the Hong Kong container terminal lasting exactly a month. Renamed *Huaying 391*, she was sent to serve at Donghai Bureau.

▲ Ballyglass; at moorings, August 1995.
(Nicholas Leach)

▼ Calshot: on exercise in the Solent,
January 2005. (Nicholas Leach)

52-46

Duke of Atholl

OFFICIAL NUMBER
1160

YEAR BUILT
1989

BUILDER
Hull by Halmatic Ltd, fit out
by William Osborne Ltd,
Littlehampton

YARD NO
WO 3269

WEIGHT
31 tons

COST
£614,659.74

DONOR
Bequest of Sir David Robinson

STATIONS
Relief Fleet
12 May 1990 – Aug 2003
(232/57)
Hartlepool
11 Aug 2003 – Sep 2004
(27/0)
Relief Fleet
27 Sep 2004 – Dec 2007 (4/0)

DISPOSAL
Sold out of service in Dec 2007
to ICE-SAR Iceland

The last Arun to be built was allocated to the Relief Fleet, but with the RNLI rapidly replacing Aruns from about 2005 she only had a career of seventeen years with the Institution. Her hull left Halmatic in February 1989 and was taken to William Osborne for fitting out. She was launched at Littlehampton on 30 October 1989 and underwent self-righting trials during November. Final trials took place in January 1990 and she passed her acceptance and forty-hour trials during February 1990.

She left Osborne's yard on 4 April 1990 and was taken to the RNLI Depot at Poole for further trials before heading north to Buckie, leaving Poole on 23 April and arriving at her destination four days later. She remained at Jones' yard, Buckie, until 10 May, when she was taken south to Dundee for her naming ceremony.

Provided from the bequest of Sir David Robinson, she was named *Duke of Atholl* to mark the ten years the Duke served as Chairman of the RNLI before his retirement in 1989. The naming ceremony was held at Dundee Docks on 12 May 1990 with Broughty Ferry lifeboat 52-09 *Spirit of Tayside* and the RNR vessel HMS *Archer* both in attendance. T. Mitchell JP, Lord Provost of Dundee, opened proceedings by welcoming the RNLI, and noting that the crew manning the new lifeboat had given collectively 160 years service at their stations of Broughty Ferry, Aberdeen, Aith and Arbroath. After a service of dedication by the Rev W. B. R. Macmillan and the Rev T. P. Robertson, His Grace named the lifeboat *Duke of Atholl*.

After her naming, *Duke of Atholl* went south to Ramsgate, arriving there on 15 May 1990, and was present alongside Festival Pier on the Thames for the RNLI's Annual General

Meeting in London on 22 May 1990 before she departed to escort the Little Ships for the fiftieth anniversary of the evacuation of the BEF from Dunkirk, towing a number of the veteran craft to safety. She was at Dover from 24 to 28 May 1990, and then returned to the RNLI Depot at Poole to take up her Relief duties.

During a seventeen-year career in the Relief Fleet, *Duke of Atholl* served at a great many of the Arun stations in the UK and a couple in Ireland. She was at Hartlepool from August 2003 to September 2004 on temporary station duty, but apart from that was used entirely as a Relief lifeboat.

One of the most difficult services in which she was involved took place on 19 November 1996 when she was serving at Newhaven. She launched to the 9,000-ton merchant vessel *Robin*, which had lost engine power seven miles off Beachy Head. Although the vessel had two anchors down, she was dragging towards the coast. The lifeboat, at reduced speed because of the atrocious conditions, took over an hour to reach the scene.

Robin had already dragged for two miles by the time the lifeboat arrived, but eventually her anchors held. The lifeboat then stood by in the heavy seas while *Robin's* crew restarted the engines. Although a hydraulic problem with the windlass delayed them for another two hours, at 6pm *Robin* was able to get under way, escorted by the lifeboat for an hour.

Duke of Atholl was sold out of service in 2007 to ICE-SAR for further service as a lifeboat in Iceland, becoming one of the last Aruns to leave RNLI service. She was shipped to Iceland in December 2007 to serve at the Isafjörður station on the north coast replacing 52-13 and also taking her name, *Gunnar Friðriksson*.

▲ Newhaven: putting out on exercise, October 1996. (Nicholas Leach)

▼ Hartlepool: putting out on exercise, September 2004. (Tony Denton)

Part Three
Aruns after service

The Aruns started to be replaced during the 1990s and, having reached the end of their RNLI service lives, were placed on the sale list and sold out of service.

The majority was sold to lifeboat and rescue organisations abroad, with a good number going to both China and Iceland, where they continue to give good service. A handful remain in private hands in British waters, used as pilot, work or pleasure boats, but only one, the third of the class, *Edward Bridges (C.S. and P.O. No.37*, was preserved and is displayed at Chatham.

This section provides information about what has happened to most (but not all) of the Aruns since leaving RNLI service. None has been heavily converted externally, although all have been modified in one way or another with minor alterations and new liveries.

▶ 52-01 was sold in October 1997 to engineering firm LADCO, of Dundee, who renamed her Arun Adventurer and based her in Dundee Docks for use promoting the firm around the UK. She also spent time at Broughty Ferry and also visited at times Arbroath, where she is pictured in June 2010. (Cliff Crone)

▶ 52-02 was sold out of service on 24 February 1998 to T. Gill and C. P. McGuinness, renamed Our Lady, and kept at Fleetwood by her new owners. In 2001 she was sold to a London owner and renamed Theocrat. Offered for sale again in 2002, she was kept around the Solent area at Bursledon and Port Solent until September 2005, when John O'Regan bought her and took her to Cork in Ireland. He kept her at East Ferry, Cork Harbour, and Kinsale, and she was renamed Samuel K. (Tony Denton)

◄ 54-03 was withdrawn from service in 1994 and in 1995 was taken to Chatham for display at the Historic Dockyard as part of the Historic Lifeboat Collection. The only Arun lifeboat to be preserved for display, she is maintained by a team of dedicated volunteers who work on all the historic lifeboats in the collection at Chatham. (Nicholas Leach)

◄ 54-04 was sold on 5 May 1999 to the Finnish Lifeboat Service, Suomen Meripelastusseura, and was renamed PR Mac Elliott. She was based at Porkkala, twenty miles west of Helsinki. (Supplied by John Pagni)

◄ 54-05 was sold on 27 October 1998 to ICE-SAR, the National Lifesaving Association of Iceland, and sailed from Buckie on 11 November 1998 to Grindavík, Iceland, via Thorshavn (Faroes), Eidj (North Faroes), Höfn (Iceland) and Heimaey (Iceland). She was renamed Oddur V. Gíslason and placed on station at Grindavík in November 1998. In 2007 she was replaced at Grindavík by 52-030 and was reallocated to Sandgerði, where she is pictured, having been renamed Hannes Þ. Hafstein after a former director of the National Life-Saving Association of Iceland. (Nicholas Leach)

► 54-06 was sold on 16 July 1998 to Cuerpo de Volantarios de los Botes Salvavidas de Valparaiso, Chile, for £55,000 and shipped free of charge to Chile via Liverpool, aboard the Hamburg Sud container ship Veruda. In Chile, she was renamed Capitan Eduardo Simpson Roth and serves as a lifeboat based at Valparaiso. (Suppled by Tony Denton)

► 54-07 was sold on 22 October 1998 to a buyer in the West Midlands and has been much travelled since. She remained unaltered as a pleasure boat at Southampton, where she is pictured, renamed Lady Arun for a number of years. In May 2003 she left Southampton for Gloucester Dock and was kept on the river Severn in the Worcester area. After a further sale, she was taken to Mountbatten Marina, near Plymouth having been converted internally at a cost of more than £80,000. In 2006 she was taken to Sweden as a yacht tender after a refit at Penzance and was renamed Solidian. (Nicholas Leach)

► 52-08 was sold in June 2002 to ICE-SAR, the National Lifesaving Association of Iceland, stationed at Rif, in Iceland's south-west corner, and renamed Björg. She is pictured at sea off Rif's small harbour in September 2010. (Nicholas Leach)

◄ 52-09 was sold on 30 May 1999 to the Royal Volunteer Coastal Patrol, Australia. She was renamed PV Danial Thain and stationed in Port Stephens for deployment by the Port Stephens Division, Australia. (Mick Prendergast)

◄ 52-10 was sold in March 2002 to ICE-SAR, the National Lifesaving Association of Iceland, and was renamed Ásgrímur S. Björnsson after a former coxswain at Reykjavik, Iceland's capital. She was placed in service at Reykjavík in June 2002, replacing another former RNLI lifeboat, Grace Paterson Ritchie (ON.988), and is pictured on exercise off Reykjavik port in September 2010. (Nicholas Leach)

◄ 52-11 was sold in June 2002 to Australia and was shipped from Poole that month. Based at The Spit, Mosman, in Sydney's Middle Harbour as part of the RVCP fleet, she was renamed P&O Nedlloyd Encounter and used as a floating classroom for the Australian Maritime College, as well as being available for SAR duties. In 2006 she was relocated from Sydney to Ulladulla in New South Wales.

► 52-12 was sold in May 2001 to the Finnish Lifeboat Service, Suomen Meripelastusseura, and left Poole on 19 May 2001 for her new home. She was stationed at Turku and renamed Arvinsilma, but in 2002 was replaced by another lifeboat which took that name in 2004. She was subsequently stationed at Hanko, and renamed PR Russarö. (By courtesy of John Pagni)

► 52-13 was sold on 18 August 2000 to ICE-SAR, the National Lifesaving Association of Iceland, and was taken there on board a container ship, which left Immingham on 23 September 2000. Renamed Gunnar Friðriksson, until December 2007 she was stationed at Ísafjörður, where she is pictured. She was replaced by 52-46 (ON.1160) and was then used as a relief boat for the other Aruns in Iceland, being kept for most of the time at the small harbour in Njarðvik, to the south of Reykjavik, having been renamed Jon Oddgeir. (Gary Markham)

► 52-14 was sold in September 1999 to A. McGreal, of Osprey Aviation Ltd, and taken to Weymouth with 'SB 1062' on her wheelhouse, to be used for training by Osprey Aviation. She was used as a safety boat at Portland Harbour operating out of Weymouth. In 2003 she was moved to Exeter, and operated out of Dartmouth. She was then moved to the Solent, and was used as a training boat at Southampton and Portsmouth. In 2008 she was sold to Montrose Harbour Authority who converted her into the pilot boat Mare Rose, as pictured. (Martin Fish)

◄ 52-16 was sold on 15 July 2003 to ICE-SAR, the National Lifesaving Association of Iceland, but en route to Iceland came free from the motor vessel Skaftarfell, on board which she was being transported, and was wrecked. The remains were found three days later on a rocky beach in Iceland. The only item found to be usable was the inflatable Y boat, although that was holed. The engines showed where the boat stranded and scattered debris was found in all directions, even on land. She is pictured in Immingham being loaded on board Skaftarfell. (Supplied by Tony Denton)

◄ 52-17 was sold in February 2003 to Tenby Marine Services and, renamed Maximus, was used as safety boat at Pendine range. She was based at Tenby and Milford Haven Marina, where she is pictured. She was sold in 2006 having remained unmodified, and was taken to South Woodham Ferrers in Essex and placed on a mooring off the north bank of the river Crouch near to Brandy Hole Yacht Club between Hullbridge and Fambridge, to be used for bird watching trips. (Nicholas Leach)

◄ 52-18 was sold in 2003 to Brian A. Angliss of Guernsey and taken to Tilbury, via Ramsgate on 26 April 2003, to be shipped to New Zealand. She has since been kept at Tutukaka Marina, 100 miles north of Auckland. She was placed at the disposal of the New Zealand Coast Guard for rescue work, while also being used as a dive boat, and was named 52-18.

► 52-19 was sold in October 2002 to the Finnish Lifeboat Service and since 2003 has been based at Kaskinen, a small village in west Finland, between Vaasa and Pori. She was renamed PR Torbay and operates with a, Atlantic 21, named PV Orion, and also bought from the RNLI. (John Pagni)

► 52-20 (pictured) and 52-15 were sold on 30 April 2003 to SANAS, Madeira and taken to Madeira on a P&O Nedlloyd container vessel in November 2003. They were then placed on hard standing at the freeport area of Caniçal at the far eastern tip of Madeira, awaiting permission from the government to be operated as rescue boats. In 2009 52-20, renamed Salvador-Do-Mar, was put in the water while protracted negotiations with the Portuguese authorities continued to gain permission to operate them as rescue boats out of Funchal or Santa Cruz.

► 52-21 was sold on 15 July 2003 to ICE-SAR, the National Lifesaving Association of Iceland, and was placed on station at Hafnarfjörður, a port just south of Reykjavik, in August 2003. She was renamed Einar Sigurjónsson after a president of National Life-Saving Association of Iceland in the 1990s. (Nicholas Leach)

◄ 52-24 was sold in March 2004 to Strathclyde Joint Police Board and, after a survey at Souter Shipyard in Cowes, was taken to the Clyde for use as a police boat, having been renamed Strathclyde. She was moored at Great Harbour, Greenock, and carried a yellow livery. In November 2008 she was sold to Andy Iannetta, who brought her to Portishead, where she was based in the Marina Yacht Haven and her name reverted to Mabel Alice (pictured). She was used for pleasure trips in the Bristol Channel and further afield. (Nicholas Leach)

◄ 52-25 was sold out of service in August 2003 to the Finnish Lifeboat Service, Suomen Meripelastusseura. She was placed on station at Kemi having been renamed PR Hebe. Along with the other Aruns sold to Finland, she was adapted for the country's colder climate by having improved heating installed in the wheelhouse. (Supplied by John Pagni)

◄ 52-26 was written off by the RNLI after being damaged on 9 September 2001, when on station at Rosslare Harbour, and was sold as scrap from Holyhead Boatyard in February 2003. She was bought by a Holyhead owner, who repaired her at the local marina, and equipped her as a fishing trip boat operating out of Holyhead. She was renamed Irish Mist and had her superstructure painted grey, and was kept at various moorings in Holyhead harbour. (Nicholas Leach)

► 52-29 was sold to the Finnish Lifeboat Service, Suomen Meripelastusseura, in autumn 2002. Renamed PR Janne Malén, she has been stationed in the west coast town of Uusikaupunki on the Gulf of Bothnia since 2003. (Supplied by John Pagni)

► After her service at Aith, 52-030 was used as a training boat numbered TL-01 by the RNLI, operating out of Poole. In October 2007 she was sold to ICE-SAR, the National Lifesaving Association of Iceland, and left the RNLI Depot at Poole on 8 October 2007 by road for shipping via Immingham. In Iceland she replaced the Arun 54-05 at the Grindavík station in the south west and was renamed Oddur V. Gíslason after a priest who served at the town in the late nineteenth century and who was very interested in sea survival. (Nicholas Leach)

► 52-31 was placed on the sale list in July 2004 and sold in July 2005 to the lifeboat service in the Faroe Islands. She became a lifeboat at Klaksvik from August 2005 and was renamed Ziska. She is pictured at Lowestoft on 28 July 2005 having been given her new livery ready for service in the Faroes. (Peter Edey)

◄ 52-32 (nearest camera) and 52-33 painted grey at Seagleam yard, Fishbourne, awaiting sale, on 24 August 2004. Both were subsequently sold to the China Rescue & Salvage Bureau, and stationed at Dalian, Beihai Bureau. 52-32 became Huaying 395 and 52-33 became Huaying 394. The numbers are reversed because China numbers move backwards, so 395 comes before 394. Both boats went to the same location for service. (Peter Edey)

◄ 52-34 was sold in December 2004 to ICE-SAR, the National Lifesaving Association of Iceland, and in early 2005 was placed on station at Höfn on the south-east coast, having been renamed Ingibjörg.
(By courtesy of ICE-SAR)

◄ 52-35 was sold in March 2004 to ICE-SAR, the National Lifesaving Association of Iceland. She was renamed Hafbjörg and placed on station at Neskaupstaður in May 2004.
(Supplied by Tony Denton)

► 52-38 was sold in November 2005 to ICE-SAR, the National Lifesaving Association of Iceland, and was stationed at Vopnafjörður after being renamed Sveinbjörn Sveinsson. She was shipped to Iceland in January 2006. (Supplied by Tony Denton)

► 52-39 was sold in 2006 to ICE-SAR, the National Lifesaving Association of Iceland, and left the RNLI Depot at Poole in September 2006. Renamed Vörður II, she was stationed at Patreksfjörður on the west coast, a station founded in 2004, and replaced a former KNRM (Netherlands) lifeboat. (Nicholas Leach)

► 52-40 was sold in October 2004 to ICE-SAR, the National Lifesaving Association of Iceland, and was placed at Skagaströnd on Iceland's north coast in early 2005 after being renamed Húnabjörg. (Nicholas Leach)

◄ 52-42 was sold in 2005 to ICE-SAR, the National Lifesaving Association of Iceland, and was stationed at Siglufjörður on the north coast. She was renamed Sigurvin and replaced a former DGzRS German rescue cruiser. She was shipped to Iceland in January 2006 and took up her operational duties shortly afterwards. (Nicholas Leach)

◄ 52-44 was sold in 2007 to China Rescue & Salvage Bureau and shipped from Felixstowe to China in mid-July. The ship left England on 18 July 2007 and took exactly one month to get to Hong Kong. The lifeboat was renamed Huaying 390 and served at Waigaoqiao Base, Donghai Bureau. She is pictured off Harwich on 16 July 2007, prior to being shipped out of Felixstowe. (Peter Edey)

◄ 52-46 was sold in December 2007 to ICE-SAR, the National Lifesaving Association of Iceland, and shipped north in the same month. She replaced the Arun 52-13 (ON.1061) at Ísafjörður, on Iceland's north-west coast, was renamed Gunnar Friðriksson, and took up her duties there in March 2008. (Nicholas Leach)

Appendix One
Arun lifeboat summary

Op No	Name	In service	Last RNLI station	Replacement	2011 location
52-01	Arun	1971–1997	Barry Dock	Arun 52-23	Dundee Docks, private owner
52-02	Sir William Arnold	1973–1998	St Peter Port	Severn 17-04	Kinsale, private owner
54-03	Edward Bridges (C.S. & P.O. No.37)	1975–1994	Torbay	Arun 52-19	The Lifeboat Collection, Chatham
54-04	Tony Vandervell	1976–1999	Weymouth	Arun 52-18	Finland Lifeboat Service
54-05	B. P. Forties	1976–1998	Aberdeen	Arun 52-39	ICE-SAR, lifeboat in Iceland
54-06	The Gough-Ritchie	1976–1998	Port St Mary	Trent 14-26	Chilean Lifeboat Society
54-07	City of Bradford IV	1977–1998	Tobermory	Arun 52-41	Sweden, private owner
52-08	Joy and John Wade	1977–2001	Yarmouth	Severn 17-25	ICE-SAR, lifeboat in Iceland
52-09	Spirit of Tayside	1978–1999	Broughty Ferry	Arun 52-29	RVCP, Australia
52-10	Soldian	1978–2001	Achill	Trent 14-28	ICE-SAR, lifeboat in Iceland
52-11	Elizabeth Ann	1979–2002	Falmouth	Severn 17-02	RVCP, Australia
52-12	Walter and Margaret Couper	1979–2001	Campbeltown	Severn 17-19	Finland Lifeboat Service
52-13	George and Olive Turner	1979–2000	Tynemouth	Severn 17-20	ICE-SAR, lifeboat in Iceland
52-14	Edith Emilie	1980–1999	Relief Fleet	—	Montrose, pilot boat
52-15	Hyman Winstone	1980–2002	Larne	Trent 14-30	SANAS, Madeira
52-16	Richard Evans (Civil Service No.39)	1981–2003	Portrush	Severn 17-23	Wrecked on way to Iceland
52-17	Sir Max Aitken	1981–2002	Relief Fleet	—	River Crouch, private owner
52-18	Robert Edgar	1981–2002	Weymouth	Severn 17-32	New Zealand, private owner
52-19	Marie Winstone	1981–2002	Torbay	Severn 17-28	Finland Lifeboat Service
52-20	Duchess of Kent	1982–2002	Relief Fleet	—	SANAS, Madeira
52-21	Davina and Charles Matthews Hunter	1982–2003	Mallaig	Severn 17-26	ICE-SAR, lifeboat in Iceland
52-22	Ralph and Bonella Farrant	1982–2005	Fenit	Trent 14-27	China Rescue & Salvage Bureau
52-23	Margaret Frances Love	1982–2005	Barry Dock	Arun 52-39	China Rescue & Salvage Bureau
52-24	Mabel Alice	1983–2003	Penlee	Severn 17-36	Portishead, private owner
52-25	A. J. R. and L. G. Uridge	1983–2003	Relief Fleet	—	Finland Lifeboat Service
52-26	St Brendan	1984–2001	Rosslare Harbour	Arun 52-45	Scrapped, rebuilt at Holyhead
52-27	Charles Brown	1984–2004	Buckie	Severn 17-37	China Rescue & Salvage Bureau
52-28	Sir Max Aitken II	1984–2005	Longhope	Arun 52-43	China Rescue & Salvage Bureau
52-29	Joseph Rothwell Sykes and Hilda M.	1984–2002	Broughty Ferry	Trent 14-31	Finland Lifeboat Society
52-030	Snolda	1986–2007	Aith	Severn 17-14	ICE-SAR, lifeboat in Iceland
52-31	Newsbuoy	1984–2004	Relief Fleet	—	Faroe Islands lifeboat service
52-32	Keith Anderson	1985–2006	Hartlepool	Trent 14-37	China Rescue & Salvage Bureau
52-33	City of Belfast	1985–2005	Donaghadee	Trent 14-36	China Rescue & Salvage Bureau
52-34	Margaret Russell Fraser	1986–2004	Calshot	Arun 52-45	ICE-SAR, lifeboat in Iceland
52-35	City of Dublin	1986–2003	Howth	Trent 14-33	ICE-SAR, lifeboat in Iceland
52-36	Roy and Barbara Harding	1986–2004	Castletownbere	Arun 52-42	ICE-SAR, lifeboat in Iceland
52-37	Kenneth Thelwall	1987–2003	Holyhead	Severn 17-41	China Rescue & Salvage Bureau
52-38	City of Glasgow III	1987–2005	Troon	Trent 14-38	ICE-SAR, lifeboat in Iceland
52-39	Mickie Salvesen	1988–2006	Barry Dock	Trent 14-29	ICE-SAR, lifeboat in Iceland
52-40	City of Plymouth	1987–2004	Plymouth	Severn 17-35	ICE-SAR, lifeboat in Iceland
52-41	Ann Lewis Fraser	1988–2005	Tobermory	Severn 17-39	China Rescue & Salvage Bureau
52-42	Murray Lornie	1989–2005	Castletownbere	Severn 17-44	ICE-SAR, lifeboat in Iceland
52-43	The Queen Mother	1989–2009	Longhope	Tamar 16-05	Montevideo, pilot boat
52-44	Hibernia	1989–2007	Relief Fleet	—	China Rescue & Salvage Bureau
52-45	Mabel Williams	1990–2007	Calshot	Tyne 47-037	China Rescue & Salvage Bureau
52-46	Duke of Atholl	1990–2007	Relief Fleet	—	ICE-SAR, lifeboat in Iceland

NB The column last station does not include Relief Fleet duties, except on boats built for Relief

Appendix Two
Stations served by Arun lifeboats

1 • Barry Dock
2 • St Peter Port
3 • Torbay
4 • Weymouth
5 • Aberdeen
6 • Port St Mary
7 • Humber
8 • Yarmouth
9 • Broughty Ferry
10 • Lerwick
11 • Falmouth
12 • Campbeltown
13 • Tynemouth
14 • Holyhead
15 • Ballycotton
16 • Portrush
17 • Larne
18 • St Mary's
19 • Fishguard
20 • Tobermory
21 • Mallaig
22 • Fenit

23 • Valentia
24 • Penlee
25 • Longhope
26 • Rosslare Harbour
27 • Buckie
28 • Stornoway
29 • Stromness
30 • Aith
31 • Islay (relief only)
32 • Newhaven
33 • Donaghadee
34 • Calshot
35 • Howth
36 • Galway Bay
37 • Castletownbere
38 • Troon
39 • Kirkwall
40 • Plymouth
41 • Barra Island
42 • Lochinver
43 • Thurso
44 • Achill
45 • Ballyglass
46 • Hartlepool
47 • Dunbar (relief only)
48 • Harwich (relief only)
49 • Dover (relief only)

Index

ON refers to a lifeboat's Official Number
The numbers in brackets in the stations section
of each entry refer to launches/lives saved